# A DIFFERENT KIND OF PRESIDENCY

*Books by Theodore C. Sorensen*

A Different Kind of Presidency: A Proposal for Breaking the Political Deadlock

Watchmen in the Night: Presidential Accountability After Watergate

The Kennedy Legacy

Kennedy

Decision-Making in the White House

# A DIFFERENT KIND
# OF PRESIDENCY

*A PROPOSAL FOR BREAKING*
*THE POLITICAL DEADLOCK*

## THEODORE C. SORENSEN

*A Cornelia and Michael Bessie Book*

**HARPER & ROW, PUBLISHERS,** New York
*Cambridge, Philadelphia, San Francisco, London*
*Mexico City, São Paulo, Sydney*

*For my daughter Juliet*

FIRST EDITION

*Designer: Sidney Feinberg*

ISBN: 0-06-039032-8

LIBRARY OF CONGRESS CATALOG CARD NUMBER: 83-48434

84 85 86 87 10 9 8 7 6 5 4 3 2 1

Then none was for a party—
   Then all were for the state;
Then the great man helped the poor,
   And the poor man loved the great;
Then lands were fairly portioned!
   Then spoils were fairly sold:
The Romans were like brothers
   In the brave days of old.

     Thomas Macaulay
     "Horatius at the Bridge"

# CONTENTS

# PROLOGUE

This year, the United States embarks once again upon its quadrennial Presidential Olympics. (In truth, the featured event in these Olympics, the cross-country marathon, in which the contestants must run through more than thirty states while simultaneously leaping high hurdles and hurling javelins at each other, began two years earlier.) The winner, regardless of party, will preside over a country in deep trouble. Only effective Presidential leadership can end these troubles before their consequences become irreversible. But neither party has provided such leadership for a long time. A whole generation of young Americans cannot remember life under a President whom they truly respected.

The problem is larger than Ronald Reagan. This little book is not unrelated to the 1984 Presidential election; but neither is it a campaign document supporting or opposing any political party or candidate in that election. The plan offered herein was not designed for or inspired by any one candidate; it is available to all candidates. Mr. Reagan and Reaganomics will be charged by many with having aggravated the national afflictions described herein; but those afflictions began long before the 1980 election. Unless we do something different, they will persist long beyond the 1984 election, regardless of who wins the White House.

The international and economic dangers described in this book are long-term dangers. They have grown to perilous proportions because a series of American Presidents, from both parties, has been unable to provide and sustain long-term leadership in international and domestic affairs. Regardless of whether we change the party or the person in the Oval Office, a change in approach is required.

I am reluctant to put forward an assessment of our political system and leadership so gloomy that it will swell the ranks of those pessimists, cynics and apathists who already reject all participation in that system, including even the casting of their ballots. But I am even more unwilling to accept the optimism of those in both parties who believe once again that the nomination and election of the right candidate in 1984 can in itself halt our long-term political stalemate. Such a candidate might be able to work miracles; he might receive a clear mandate; he might enjoy for four solid years solid support from a solid Congressional majority. But the history of the past decade and a half argues against any such miracles, mandate or majority.

"America," Arthur Schlesinger, Jr., wrote not so long ago, "stands at an impasse, awaiting a new burst of creativity in statecraft." This slender volume offers one possible way out of that impasse.

# PART
# I

# THE DANGERS
# OF PARTISAN EXCESS

———————

# 1

## POLITICAL GRIDLOCK

DURING the last few years, pundits, political scientists and even ex-Presidents have commented repeatedly on the "decline of the Presidency," the "imperiled Presidency," the "attrition in the Presidency," the "depleted stature and authority" of the Presidency, and our long series of "frustrated," "ineffective," "egocentric, tainted . . . and befuddled" Presidents. Not one of this country's Chief Executives since Eisenhower has served the eight years permitted by the Constitution. (Indeed, my daughter had lived under four Presidents before she was eight years old!)

We have witnessed in the last several administrations a "political ineffectiveness" cycle as relentless and as harmful to our national strength and cohesion as the ups and downs of the economic cycle. After each Presidential succession, the nation hoped and his supporters believed that a four-year period of stable, harmonious leadership and progress was at last at hand. Each of the new Presidents took office in a glow of enthusiasm and with a pledge of new solutions. Both the Congress and the opposition vowed cooperation.

But each time, the glow faded, cooperation gave way to confrontation, the new solutions sank into confusion, and newly shattered hopes swelled the tide of public cynicism. Long before his term ended, each new President had lost much if not most of his effectiveness, his authority, his credibility, and the respect in which he had initially been held in Washington and the world at large.

In all these cases, both the expectations and the disappointments have been unrealistic. Some of the same members of the press and public who at the start of his term unjustifiably idolized a new President as a savior ended up unjustifiably savaging him as an incompetent. Finley Peter Dunne's Mr. Dooley observed long ago: "Americans build their triumphal arches out of bricks—so that we will have something handy to hurl at our heroes when they invariably disappoint us." (That tradition has been strengthened in a generation nurtured on television, which generally chews up and spits out heroes and celebrities in the course of a few prime-time seasons, consigning them to reruns when their declining ratings require their replacement by a fresh set of stars.)

Some say, not without reason, that the fault lies not in ourselves but in these stars of the political firmament. It is true that each of our last several Presidents has had his particular weaknesses and peculiarities; but so do all human beings (including most of the defeated Presidential candidates over this same period). It is true that each of these Presidents was assisted in his accession to the Oval Office by unusual outside circumstances unrelated to his individual merit; but there is no such thing as a "typical" Presidential election. With the possible exception of Ronald Reagan, no one of these Presidents was deemed to be outside the mainstream of American political thought; and yet all of them in time saw their policies and programs bogged down in acrimony and antipathy.

Johnson in 1964, Nixon in 1972, and Reagan in 1980 won overwhelming public support at the polls. Johnson carried with him majorities for his party in both houses of Congress. Reagan carried with him a large majority in the Senate and an effective working majority of Republicans and "boll weevil" Democrats in the House. Nixon was an astute and experienced politician, skilled in circumscribing Congressional opposition. Kennedy and Carter enjoyed party control of the Executive Branch and both houses of Congress. Ford, though unelected, entered the Oval Office on a wave of sympathy and good wishes that cut across all partisan and ideological lines. Yet all six of them encountered in time the same diminution in effectiveness and authority.

Others say, not without reason, that this decline in Presidential effectiveness is all to the good, that the imperiled Presidency is preferable to the imperial Presidency. Clearly, in this post-Watergate era, the power of Presidential leadership cannot be unaccountable. Clearly, in this post-Vietnam era, the power of national commitment cannot be exclusively Presidential.

But neither can we afford to have those powers so

divided, so diluted, so ineffectively exercised, that this nation cannot meet its responsibilities at home or abroad. Whenever the President is unable to weld the federal government into an effective instrument of leadership, this nation suffers—and the whole world is concerned.

Our allies in particular have been concerned about America's political stalemate. Their fears have not always been expressed in private. In any organization, whether an alliance, a nation, a corporation or a family, inaction at the center produces division instead of progress. The United States, by virtue of its inherent political, financial and military power, necessarily remains at the center of Free World diplomatic and economic activity. But our leadership has been diminished. We command as much attention as ever, but less respect. We still have the ear of every Western opinion-maker, but not the confidence.

All the ills of this nation, much less all those of the Atlantic Alliance, cannot be blamed on or solved by the White House. But sustained leadership in and from the United States requires sustained leadership from the President, our only nationally elected executive, the author of our national agenda, the one person under our system whom we most expect to worry more about the next generation than about the next election. Congress can legislate, appropriate, investigate, deliberate, terminate and educate—all essential functions. But it is not organized to initiate, negotiate or act with the kind of swift and informal discretion that our changing world so often requires. Leadership can come only from the Presidency.

## CONFIDENCE AND CONSENSUS

What every American President requires if he is to lead—indeed, what every democracy and its elected officials require—can be summed up in two words: confidence and consensus.

A great nation, with sufficient confidence in its strength and purpose to act without waiting for a public opinion poll or computer printout, and with a political consensus sufficiently strong to sustain that action through criticism and self-doubt, can successfully tackle any challenge. But in the last decade and a half, both confidence and consensus have been sadly eroded in the United States.

Confidence was once a hallmark of the American character, reflected in our songs, our humor and our oratory. We were confident of our military and economic strength, our system of government, our moral integrity and our manifest destiny. We were confident that we could outfight, outproduce, outspend, out-think and even outdrink any other people on earth. We were sure we had the best schools, the most weapons, the first man on the moon, the last word in any crisis, a united Western Alliance and a constantly expanding economy. Undefeated in war, magnanimous in peace, we knew who we were and what we wanted and where we were going.

Looking back on my work with John F. Kennedy on his Inaugural Address, I realize the extent to which those words of twenty-three years ago epitomized this spirit of confidence. JFK's experience in the thousand days that followed would dampen some of his own confidence. But there was little disagreement from either political party on that snowy afternoon when he said that Americans were ready to "pay any price, bear any burden, meet any hardship, support any friend, oppose any foe, to assure the survival and success of liberty"; when he summoned them "to bear the burden of a long twilight struggle . . . against the common enemies of man: tyranny, poverty, disease and war itself"; when he urged them to ask not what their country could do for them but what they could do for their country and for world freedom.

In the words of the famous Doonesbury cartoon panel in which two young sophisticates twenty years later laugh at those very phrases and then stare mournfully at each other: "God, what happened to us?" What happened to cause those words to sound so different today?

What happened was a series of American setbacks, disappointments and humiliations, beginning only a few months after that Inaugural Address with Kennedy's own fiasco at the Bay of Pigs, which demonstrated the rapidly changing nature of a world that Americans could no longer dominate or even fully understand, much less predict.

—"Support any friend, oppose any foe" reminded us in January 1961 of the Marshall Plan's success in helping Western Europe ward off Soviet-backed insurgents, or of the heroic airlift that preserved the freedom of West Berlin; but today that phrase would raise suspicions about this country being dragged in and bogged down in Central America or the Persian Gulf in another frustrating, humiliating, divisive war like Vietnam.

—"Let us never fear to negotiate," said Kennedy. After all, the United States had led in creating a network of global and Atlantic diplomatic institutions, and in successfully negotiating with the Soviet Union for the neutrality of Austria. But the long and largely fruitless haggling with North Vietnamese negotiators, the increasing anti-American tenor of United Nations resolutions, the futility of diplomatic responses to Soviet moves against Afghanistan and Poland, and the long, humiliating confinement of our diplomats by revolutionaries in Teheran have all made many Americans cynical and diffident about diplomacy and negotiations, certainly including any such dream as the "grand and global alliance, north and south, east and west," of which Kennedy spoke.

—"Pay any price" sounded fine when we thought of our proud role after the Second World War as the only victor in history to help rebuild the nations it vanquished; but it has had less appeal in recent years to those who blame the loss of their jobs in the local automobile or steel or television plant on Japanese or German imports.

—Kennedy said he did not shrink from his awesome responsibility, but welcomed it; and thinking of Lincoln at Gettysburg or Roosevelt at Hyde Park, Americans were happy to give him Presidential authority as well as responsibility. Today, thinking of Nixon at Watergate, we suspect anyone reaching for power.

The national mood has changed, and not without reason. With persistently high rates of interest and unemployment over the past decade, families unable to find work, or unable to meet their mortgage payments, are less inclined to ask what they can do for their country, much less for world freedom. They do not want to bear any more burdens or meet any more hardships. There is hardship enough in the poverty, crime and drug abuse spreading outward from our central cities.

A great many Americans, in short—and the polls have evinced such a trend for nearly twenty years— have lost confidence: confidence in our leaders, in our government, in our political parties, even in our system. They lack confidence in government statistics and white papers, in Presidential programs and promises. Declining voter participation over the past two decades, a drop in party registration and identification, a 75 percent drop in the public's confidence in Congress, all reflect this national malaise, as Jimmy Carter termed it. Does the government respond to the needs of the public? Can Washington be trusted to do what is right most of the time? Twenty or more years ago, those questions were answered affirmatively by an overwhelming majority of the sample polled. Not now.

This decline in confidence does not apply only to disillusioned youth, dispirited welfare recipients and embittered minorities. Too many consumers have lost confidence in the government's ability to stabilize prices and the value of money over the long haul. Too many investors have lost confidence in the government's ability to hold down budget deficits and interest rates. Too many business managers doubt the government's ability to guide us successfully through this turbulent economic transition. Even many of our politicians and career government officials have lost confidence in this country's ability to accept the sacrifice and self-discipline required in today's world.

So long as this country is lacking in confidence, no President, however popular or wise he may be, can sustain for long an innovative or controversial program, however sound or essential it may be. Nor can that President rebuild public *confidence*, once undermined, unless, like Franklin Roosevelt in 1933, he is the beneficiary of a national *consensus*.

In the last year especially, "consensus" has become a favorite if elusive objective in American political speeches and commentaries. We have been told by various leaders that we cannot achieve a consistent approach to the problems of Central America without a consensus; that we cannot successfully compete abroad without a consensus; that we cannot maintain a credible military or diplomatic posture without a consensus; and that we cannot even expect the President to govern effectively without a consensus. All these statements are true. But we have no consensus.

Consensus has never meant unanimity. No modern President has ruled without opposition from both the left and the right. No modern President has proclaimed policies free from dissent. But from the end of the Second World War until approximately the third year of Lyndon Johnson's Presidency, the generally moderate majorities dominating both parties—however much they differed on means and priorities—were in broad agreement on the basic principles guiding our government's conduct.

On domestic policy, these moderates in both parties usually endorsed an activist though limited role for the federal government in helping to spread somewhat the benefits of prosperity, to seek economic justice and participation, and to reduce at least in part the incidence and impact of poverty, sickness, unemployment and environmental damage. In foreign affairs, they generally agreed on the need to prevent both nuclear war and Soviet aggression, to lead a harmonious Western Alliance, to seek international limits on nuclear and other forms of weapons, to promote international trade, and to help those struggling for dignity in the less developed nations.

That may not bear much resemblance to current American policy, either at home or abroad. But the consensus on both domestic and foreign policy—between the two parties and within each of them—collapsed long before the election of Ronald Reagan.

Here at home, the consensus in support of government social and economic intervention eroded as its costs became less acceptable and its accomplishments less clear, as the end of continuous growth in our economy and productivity coincided with a dramatic increase in the number of people (both young and female) entering the labor market, and as many a familiar landmark in the American economy vanished in a new age of internationalization and high technology in which mankind's knowledge now doubles every seven years.

The American people were told, sometimes simultaneously, that small was better and that small was elitist, that growth was essential and that growth must be limited, that what we needed most was more regulation and more deregulation, a monetary policy and a supply-side policy. Was a new "incomes policy" the only route to stability or too hot to handle politically? Should a new "industrial policy" provide preferential treatment for new technology or transitional assistance for basic industry? Liberal economists disagreed with each other as well as with conservative economists. (It was said, with good reason, that if all the economists in this country were laid end to end, they still wouldn't reach a conclusion.)

Successive administrations ricocheted from anti-inflation priorities to anti-recession priorities and back again; from deficit reduction to tax reduction; from controlling the money supply to controlling welfare expenditures to controlling interest rates. With the government's foot shifting from the gas pedal to the brake and back, usually at the wrong time and frequently at the same time, it is not surprising that our economy continued to stutter and sputter.

In foreign policy, one experience above all others—our costly, unsuccessful and often disingenuous descent into the quagmire of Vietnam—not merely ended the old consensus but shattered it into dozens of pieces in the late 1960s. Arguments over that war spread to arguments over other Third World interventions, then over U.S.–Soviet relations, then arms control, covert operations, defense appropriations, human rights, and virtually every item on the international agenda.

Divisions deepened along lines of age, gender, education, occupation, race and region as well as politics and philosophy. Bitter poisons of rancor and suspicion spread into the American body politic; and not all of them have dissipated. "The children of Vietnam," remarked one young Congressman during an angry 1983 debate, "are the adults of El Salvador." The result has been an American foreign policy with more inconsistency and less continuity, more spokesmen and less predictability, alarming our allies, antagonizing our adversaries and confusing the world.

In theory, broad support remains in this country for a foreign policy that advocates both defending freedom and negotiating peaceful solutions. But in practice, many Americans remain suspicious of any justification for U.S. military intervention other than hostile forces landing on Coney Island, and others remain suspicious of any pact with the Soviets in which they do not agree to turn over to us the keys to their national arsenal, treasury and liquor cabinet.

In theory, no one embraces a return to isolationism. But in practice, many Americans are fully supportive of this country's playing an effective role in world affairs only so long as it does not require us to consult meaningfully with our allies, send money to developing countries, send troops anywhere, send or even sell arms to anyone, compete with imports or investments from other nations, respect the United Nations, or accept any special burden not imposed on every other member of the Western Alliance, including Luxembourg and Iceland.

The 1980 Report of the President's Commission for a National Agenda for the Eighties noted "an increasing inability on the part of Americans to form effective coalitions for the general good." That is a masterpiece of understatement. When the President's authority declines, other centers of power—Congressional subcommittee chairmen, senior civil servants, top military brass, Cabinet members and White House aides—set out on their own, express their own views, plant their own stories, build their own bases. They cannot effectively lead the nation; but they can, by moving into the vacuum created by weakened Presidential leadership, weaken that leadership still further.

Under those circumstances, coordination by the President of Executive Branch advice, actions and particularly statements, even coordination of his own Cabinet and White House aides, becomes increasingly difficult. Battles for turf or influence between rival administration factions, and competition for the President's soul or favor between ideologues and pragmatists, spill over into the press, into Presidential travel arrangements, into decisions on who is invited to meetings and who keeps the minutes, even into the post-Administration memoirs of the participants. (Apparently, victory in these disputes is determined not by which Presidential adviser gave the sounder advice but by whose book received the most publicity.) A President may try to incorporate into his pronouncements and policies the views of two conflicting factions, as did President Carter, or he may instead simply alternate between them, as does President Reagan. Either way, the result is more confusion.

In that confusion still other forces of fragmentation are chipping away: tens of thousands of political action committees, lobbyists and trade associations, each representing a particular ideological, industry or labor group, often using the pressure of campaign funds and direct mail campaigns to obtain a hand on the legislative pork barrel; single-issue organizations, unable to accept the kind of compromise that has traditionally held this country together because they have no other marbles to trade; separate political and Congressional caucuses—for women or gays, Blacks or Hispanics, tobacco interests or steel, urban areas or farm—each seeking its piece of the political pie; a veritable army of investigative journalists, Congressional sleuths and self-anointed intellectual critics, out to discredit, defeat or demean each new Administration and those who serve it. Old battles, like labor versus management, are joined by new battles, like snowbelt versus sunbelt and smokestack industry versus service industry.

In an atmosphere of disharmony and disunity, the watchword is everyone for himself; and racism, protectionism and jingoism inevitably rise. No President can successfully govern a polarized nation, a Republican Congressman observed recently. A democracy fragmented is a democracy endangered.

## CONGRESS AND COMMISSIONS

Nowhere is this lack of consensus more clearly apparent or more sharply felt than in the Congress and its relations with the last five Presidents. Consider foreign policy in particular. Presidents Truman and Eisenhower, in the age of foreign policy consensus, worked successfully with Congressional leaders to advance America's role in the world, even during periods when one

or both houses of Congress were controlled by the opposition party. President Kennedy, in his responses to
the Berlin crisis and the Cuban missile crisis, was able
simply to inform Congressional leaders without con-
sulting them, an approach that would not be tolerated
today. But many of the foreign policy initiatives of
their five successors have been blocked, assailed or
substantially altered by Congress, even during periods
when one or both houses of Congress were controlled
by the President's party.

A great power unable to fulfill its commitments will
not long be respected or trusted. During these last sixteen years, our Presidents, Secretaries of State, and
other Executive Branch officials have carefully negoti-
ated commitments to other countries that they believed the national interest required, only to see Congress water them down or wash them out. As former
Presidential counsel Lloyd Cutler has written: "We are
the only major nation whose head of government cannot commit the government he heads."

As noted in the next chapter, a long series of arms
control initiatives has been blocked by Executive-
Legislative deadlock. Who knows what our other
NATO allies thought when Congress suspended all
U.S. military shipments to Turkey? Who knows what
options in Central America might have been lost when
Congress delayed and diluted the assistance promised
by the Executive to the new revolutionary government
in Nicaragua? Who knows the long-term consequences
of Congress's blocking Presidentially pledged economic assistance to dozens of countries, trade and tax
agreements with others, arms supplies to still others,

and covert operations elsewhere? The current Foreign Assistance Act contains more than one hundred individual exceptions and restrictions added by Congress—primarily as a means, explained one member of the House Foreign Affairs Committee, of "getting the attention" of the Executive Branch.

In many of these instances, Congress, in my view, was right and the President was wrong. In others, debate, however time-consuming, was desirable or Executive Branch commitments in advance of Congressional clearance were inadvisable. Friction and inefficiency in Presidential-Congressional relations are not an aberration. On the contrary, under our Constitutional separation of powers they were intended, as Justice Brandeis wrote in a famous dissent, "to preclude exercise of arbitrary power . . . to save the people from autocracy." Power as the rival of power, whatever its drawbacks, has on the whole served us well. That basic system should not be altered.

But other countries, more accustomed to the greater continuity and predictability of one-party rule or to the merged executive-legislative power of the parliamentary system, are appalled at our Chief Executive's inability to follow through on his own international commitments. They are surprised and sometimes dismayed when the President's "final" decision does not end debate. They are resentful of the need to lobby Congress as well as the Executive Branch on aid, trade and a host of other matters.

The Government of Panama was required in effect to renegotiate the Canal Treaties with the United States Senate. That body was preparing to do the same with SALT II. To obtain AWAC aircraft, the Government of Saudi Arabia had to provide separate assurances to the Senate. It will surely occur to future U.S. negotiating partners not to use all their bargaining chips in the Wednesday night poker game with the President's envoys if they are to save some for the Saturday night game with the Senate.

To be sure, Congressional interference with Presidential initiatives in foreign affairs is not new. During those long periods of our national history when Congress was, for all practical purposes, responsible for the conduct of American foreign policy—specifically, during the last third of the nineteenth century and between the First and Second World Wars—the United States played no effective role in international affairs. Prior to the Japanese attack on Pearl Harbor, Roosevelt's limited efforts to put obstacles in the path of Hitler's aggression were largely blocked by Congress. Indeed, every President has sensed an improvement in Washington's humid, sometimes fetid, climate whenever Congress goes home. But the greater distrust of Presidential discretion and secrecy that grew out of our plunge into Vietnam and our revulsion at Watergate, combined with the steadily declining hold of our political parties on the conduct of their Congressional members, has in the past decade reduced to an all-time low the long-term influence on Congress of both the President and the party leadership.

Truman and Eisenhower could appeal to or bargain with a handful of Congressional leaders and committee chairmen and count on those bargains being honored. But power now is more widely dispersed in Congress also. An individual member, primarily concerned about his own or her own reelection, fund-raising, local newspapers and local interest groups, pays less attention to party unity and party leadership. "Everybody's a Secretary of State around here," said a Republican Congressman in 1983. "It's an exercise in power. You get a kick out of meddling in foreign policy."

Clearly, 535 members of the House and Senate, each representing a different local constituency, cannot—however wise and experienced many of them may be in foreign affairs—match the Presidency in selective foreign policy initiative, discretion and implementation. As House Majority Leader Jim Wright observed, "We can't have 535 Secretaries of State" (or, as one U.S. diplomat termed it, "535 ants sitting on a log floating down a turbulent river, each one thinking he's steering").

The role of Congress in domestic affairs is traditionally as well as Constitutionally still more pronounced. The checks and balances designed by the Framers have tried the patience of virtually every President trying to lead at home. But here, too, the lack of consensus under recent administrations has gone further than ever before in preventing any effective action on politically sensitive domestic controversies.

Almost no one in Washington, for example, Republican or Democrat, legislator or administrator, liberal or conservative, ideologue or pragmatist, doubts the urgent need to reduce sharply the $200 billion annual budget deficit. But how? Democratic Congressmen disagree with each other on cuts in the defense budget and with Republican Congressmen on cuts in the domestic budget. Both houses of Congress blocked implementation of a bill to raise revenue through withholding taxes on interest and dividends, but could not agree with each other on what new taxes to substitute. The President promised to veto any bills increasing taxes, withdrew his request for a standby tax, and even condemned the bipartisan Budget Resolution adopted by both houses last year. Meanwhile, lobbyists continue to obtain still further tax privileges and to prevent reductions in spending programs of importance to the interests they represent.

The result is all check and no balance. It is almost as if this country's policy-making process were being shaped not only by the Constitutional laws on legislation and regulation but also by the physical laws of force and counterforce. "Gridlock" is the new term applied to the urban traffic tangle in which lines of waiting vehicles blocking intersections in all directions become so long and unyielding that ultimately no one can move forward or backward. Washington in the past fifteen years, with each party and each faction within a party checking the other, with each house of Congress blocking the other, with each branch of government curbing the other, and with myriad special-interest groups on the left and the right delaying and belaboring them all, has increasingly been in a state of political gridlock. Political analyst and former Presidential aide Horace Busby, noting the increasing malfunctioning of our governmental institutions due to excesses of partisanship, added: "On critical national decisions, such as those about budget policy, Congress, in particular, has come close to ruinous stalemate because partisan political interests have transcended the national interest."

Each of our last several Presidents has tried on occasion to appeal over the heads of recalcitrant members of Congress, hoping their constituents will apply the necessary pressure. Such efforts rarely succeed. Members of Congress, elected without regard to their respective party's Presidential candidate, feel relatively immune to his political wrath. They know little and care less about his commitments and platform. Typically they had little to do with his nomination and campaign; most of them hardly know him; and only rarely have they served with him in national office. During the last sixty years, only one sitting member of Congress (Kennedy) has been elected President, and only two others (Goldwater and McGovern) were even nominated by major parties.

Each of our last several Presidents has also sought on occasion to break the cycle of Executive-Legislative gridlock by invoking the spirit of bipartisanship. Eloquently worded to appeal to national unity, most of these invocations can be translated to read simply: "Support me, your President."

Congressional and opposition leaders sometimes respond to such Presidential appeals with a little bipartisan tune of their own, which stripped of its rhetorical flourishes reads: "Only to the extent that you get the blame if things go wrong."

The supposed tradition of a bipartisan foreign policy, so prevalent in the 1940s, has been largely a myth over the last two decades—a concept selectively invoked by each President in need of support and conveniently forgotten by his party when it is returned to the opposition role—a game in which each party hopes to pin responsibility on the other for some future disaster or current impasse—an artifice by which controversial decisions can be avoided, delayed or obscured.

It is unrealistic to expect consistent bipartisan support for any President so long as the opposition party in this country is unable to speak with one voice. Its ideologues never trust the man in the White House. Its pragmatists never want to look like a pale carbon copy of the Administration. According to the late Senator Robert A. Taft, Sr., who disliked the way his fellow Republican Senator Arthur Vandenberg cooperated with Roosevelt and Truman, the duty of the opposition is to oppose.

The opening weeks of the Ninety-eighth Congress in January 1983 illustrate the problem. The Republican President in his State of the Union Address to the Congress called for bipartisan harmony. The Democratic Speaker of the House solemnly declared: "The American people want action, not partisan bickering." The Republican Majority Leader of the Senate responded in kind. Cooperation prevailed on a jobs bill in the House and a Social Security compromise in the Senate. Both parties joined on legislation for new highways and gasoline taxes. But soon, with but a few notable exceptions, they were at each other's throats.

The President condemned a bipartisan plan on spending that would have cut his defense budget. Democratic Congressmen condemned a Republican plan that would have cut domestic programs. A *New*

*York Times* editorial condemned the very concept of bipartisan trust in "a President who has heaped mistrust on predecessors in both parties." Any consensus on such emotional and politically sensitive issues as a nuclear freeze or El Salvador was out of the question. A halt to partisan attacks on a President perceived to be running hard for reelection, any acceptance on faith that his every move was not politically motivated, were also out of the question.

President Reagan, casting about for a different approach, rediscovered another old Presidential ploy in the bipartisan consensus game—the Presidential blue-ribbon commission.

From time to time, an Executive-Legislative deadlock on a specific short-term issue can be successfully broken by a Presidential commission that is genuinely bipartisan, independent of Presidential control, and composed largely of experienced former officials whose combined stature and expertise are sufficient to enable them to talk frankly with each other, disagree with the President, party leaders, and powerful interest groups, find (with input from both President and Congress) a consensus that had eluded them both, and win the confidence of the public. The "package" recommendations of such a commission offer both parties and both branches of government a legitimate way to compromise in a face-saving fashion, reduce political heat and achieve progress. The 1982–83 Commission on Social Security, with members appointed by both the President and Congressional leaders, filled that role admirably.

But commissions whose members are picked solely

by the White House to achieve a particular result—to endorse a Presidential policy, to buy time, to evade responsibility or to obscure the President's actions—are at best cheerleaders, not impartial experts. That is not always bad. Such a commission often presents a useful means of obtaining distinguished outside support for such politically unappetizing necessities as increases in foreign aid or official compensation.

But cheerleading commissions rarely produce bipartisan consensus in the Congress and the country. President Reagan's MX Commission on Strategic Forces, although distinguished and bipartisan in membership, contained no opponent of that controversial weapons system and considered no alternatives to it. His Kissinger Commission on Central America, also distinguished and bipartisan, contained none of the outspoken experts known to oppose his military focus on that region (in sharp contrast to the type of commission urged by the Republican and Democratic Senators who had sought its establishment).

Moreover, caution is in order regarding the excessive use of this device. (Blue-ribbon panels have recently been established or urged to decide U.S. policy on hunger, taxes, deficits, the defense budget, strategic doctrine, teachers' pay, medical care and groundwater purification.) This country cannot be governed by even genuinely independent and knowledgeable bipartisan commissions. Useful on a few narrowly defined and immediate issues, they cannot cope with continuing large-scale problems over a long period of time in which facts and circumstances change rapidly. Even well-intentioned commissions often produce politically unrealistic, practically unenforceable or deliberately imprecise recommendations. They cannot be a substitute for the political judgment of elected officials accountable to the public and responsible under the Constitution. They dilute still further the authority of departments and agencies established by the Congress and staffed by career experts.

Hugh Sidey, noting in his weekly *Time* magazine column on the Presidency the disturbing similarities between today's political turbulence and that which preceded the Civil War, summed it up well: "[A] paralyzing partisanship is stronger today than at any other time in the past 30 years. . . . [T]he resort to . . . yet another Presidential commission . . . represents an admission of political gridlock." It is that systemic condition of paralysis that must be corrected if we are ever to regain our national confidence and fulfill our national promise.

# 2

## TIME IS RUNNING OUT

INEFFECTIVENESS in Washington is not new. Our recent Presidents are not the first to find their authority diminished and their proposals impeded. The country has survived this kind of Washington power outage in previous eras. But this time the national problems not being adequately addressed are so deep-seated and far-reaching that the irreversible consequences of continuing drift could drastically alter our national future. Specifically:

- If we do not in the next five years reach an agreement with the Soviet Union halting the nuclear arms race, both superpowers will undertake strategic weapon developments and deployments that will make any meaningful limitation impossible and future confrontations unavoidable.
- If we do not in the next five years drastically reduce our federal deficits, this country's national debt and annual borrowing will grow to levels so disproportionate to the size of our economy and Budget as to be unsupportable.

- If we do not in the next five years begin to restore the ability of American industry to compete internationally, our prospects for regaining world economic leadership, steady growth and high employment will be indefinitely lost.
- If we do not in the next five years develop with our allies and the international finance institutions a long-term restructuring of Third World debt, a wave of government bankruptcies or debt repudiations will undermine the U.S. banking system and with it much of our economy and that of the Western world.
- If we do not in the next five years establish with our industrial allies fair and enforceable rules on trade barriers, subsidies, credits and exchange rates, a rising tide of protectionism and commercial warfare will wash away the institutional channels for trade expansion, painstakingly built over three decades, on which world prosperity is dependent.
- If we do not in the next five years develop with the Government of Mexico a series of agreements on trade, immigration, credit, energy, population and economic development, assuring the economic and political stability of that nation, we will for the first time in this century face a serious security problem on our own border.

No doubt this list is incomplete. No doubt other national and international problems will reach such perilous proportions in the next five years that failure to act will risk unacceptable consequences for our country. But this list is long enough—long enough to make us realize that we cannot go on as we are.

Every one of these problems is a political minefield that no political party and no branch of government can dare to cross alone. Not one of these problems can be solved without incurring the wrath of one or more powerful voices in our society. Not one is close to solution today.

Let us examine in more detail the first three problems cited, for their urgency cannot be doubted: the need to curb the nuclear arms race, the need to reduce our Budget deficits, and the need to restore our competitive position in the world economy.

*

The grim facts of the nuclear arms race are widely known and rarely disputed. Only a brief summary is required to remind us all that the failure of the superpowers to curb this spiral is irresponsible in the extreme.

The United States and the Soviet Union now possess in combined nuclear destruction capability the equivalent of three million bombs like the one that gutted Hiroshima—the equivalent of four tons of TNT for every person on earth. Each of these two superpowers now deploys more than seven thousand air-, land- and sea-based strategic nuclear warheads. The United States has more total warheads; the Soviets have more total megatonnage. They have more submarine missile launchers; we have more warheads on each launcher. We have more cruise missiles and bombers; they have more powerful land-based missiles. Each nuclear weapons system or delivery system newly developed by one side has inevitably begotten, usually within a few years, a comparable means of destruction on the other side.

Each side long ago passed the level of minimum deterrence—the level necessary to assure a force large enough and diverse enough to ride out an enemy first strike and still be able to destroy the attacker. Each side continues to build and deploy more nuclear weapons in excess of potential targets and conceivable need. More dangerously, each is in the process of deploying nuclear weapons where they have never before been deployed. Each is moving into the production of massive but vulnerable hair-trigger weapons that must be quickly fired on warning lest they be destroyed—or, conversely, quickly destroyed by an attacking force lest they be fired. Each is increasing its arsenal of missiles with multiple warheads or mobile bases that will make it more difficult for the other to compare force levels and verify any agreed-upon reduction. If the nuclear arms race is ever to be halted, time is running out.

But there is no sign of a halt, no reduction, not even significant negotiations. Each side says it is up to the other to change its attitude. Neither offers arms limitations it believes the other can accept; neither listens seriously to the other's proposals. Each sees the other's offers as either propaganda or one-sided or both. Each sees the other's arms buildup, even when undertaken in response to its own, as evidence of a desire for superiority.

The American people neither know nor trust the

Soviet Union. Many fear or hate its totalitarian sup-
pression of domestic dissent, its domination of its
neighbors and its support of revolutions abroad. We
cannot ignore our very real differences with the Soviet
Union; but we cannot in the nuclear age resolve those
differences by combat. The balance of military power
that both sides desire can more safely and economically be achieved by verifiable arms control agreements than by an unrestrained arms race. The secrecy
practiced by the U.S.S.R., and the virtually absolute
security it seems to seek for itself, make any significant
agreement between our two governments difficult at
best. But the inability of the American government to
break through its own political deadlock on this issue
has made impossible on our part the kind of coherent,
consistent approach required to bargain meaningfully.

Each of our last several Presidents has put forward
his own nuclear arms control proposal, different in important ways from that of his predecessor. Each of
these administrations has spoken with more than one
voice on the nature of the U.S.–Soviet relationship.
Each of these Presidents has encountered opposition
from both Congress and his own party on the future
direction of that relationship. The result: stalemate.

As President Reagan's MX Commission on Strategic
Forces reported in 1983:

> For the last decade, each successive Administration has
> made proposals for arms control of strategic offensive
> systems that have become embroiled in political con-
> troversy. . . . None has produced a ratified treaty . . . ,
> agreement among ourselves, restraint by the Soviets or
> lasting mutual limitations.

—When one President offered the Soviets equal access to the U.S. import market—"most favored nation" trading status—as an inducement to moderate their behavior and facilitate arms limitation agreement, Congress blocked it.

—When two Presidents reached agreement with the Soviets on separate arms control treaties limiting underground nuclear tests and peaceful nuclear explosives, Congress stalled both treaties; subsequent Presidents adhered to their provisions but never pushed for ratification.

—When one President's negotiators neared agreement with the Soviets on the comprehensive nuclear test ban sought by his four predecessors, his reelection campaign appeared to take precedence; his successor in office suspended those negotiations indefinitely.

—When one President reached agreement with the Soviets on a very modest treaty for the limitation of strategic weapons—SALT II—Congress stalled it; then the President deferred it; then his successor attacked it; then he said he would live up to it so long as the Soviets did; then he hinted that they had not.

—When one President sought a new massive weapons system, the MX, as a means of getting the Soviets seriously to the bargaining table, Congress tentatively approved its initial funding—but primarily as a means of getting that President seriously to the bargaining table.

—When the House of Representatives adopted a resolution calling for both superpowers to join in a verifiable freeze on nuclear weapons, the President denounced the proposal and the Senate dropped it.

—When that President scheduled the retirement of our accident-prone, use-or-lose Titan II nuclear missiles, Congress—including some of those most vociferously advocating a nuclear freeze—blocked it.

—When a bipartisan group in the Senate urged a "build-down" approach to reducing the quantity while still improving the quality of nuclear weapons, the President damned it with faint praise, long study and a barely comprehensible version of his own.

The responses of Soviet negotiators throughout this period have rarely been encouraging—but to what policy are they expected to respond? The longtime Soviet Foreign Minister, Andrei Gromyko, whose never-changing countenance faces an ever-changing array of United States Secretaries of State—at one time four of them in little more than two years—knows this country better than most of his isolated Kremlin colleagues know it. But he cannot know our position if we don't.

Secretary of State Shultz, referring to "fifteen years in which foreign policy has been increasingly a divisive issue," called last year for "a durable political consensus at home and within the Atlantic Alliance on the nature of the Soviet challenge." But our own lack of consensus and consistency disturbs our Atlantic allies. Former West German Chancellor Helmut Schmidt commented sourly on the number of "American U-turns" regarding medium-range nuclear weapons in Europe. Our allies favor a strong Western defense and deterrent, but they want them accompanied by détente. Their people are understandably frightened by our loose political rhetoric about Soviet superiority, about the West fighting and winning a nuclear war, and about no compromising with evil.

There is reason enough to be frightened. No expert predicts a nuclear war this year or next. The superpowers will be too cautious for that, despite their bluster. But if World War III ever comes, it is unlikely to have been predicted by any expert. It will not begin like World War II, carefully planned and deliberately launched by a malevolent aggressor. It is more likely to begin like World War I, by a spark from a single match mindlessly struck by a minor player, spreading slowly, spontaneously, then suddenly out of control in a world already made combustible by the accumulation of deadly weapons.

War between the superpowers would not for long, if ever, be confined to conventional forces. A nuclear war between the superpowers would not for long, if ever, be confined to tactical weapons or to outer space or to selected military targets or to the European continent. We can forget the absurd talk about distributing shovels, evacuating cities and "winning" what's left of our planet. We can forget the fond hopes for a futuristic "Star Wars" defense or another Cuban missile withdrawal.

Some say that no one will ever dare defy a nuclear superpower. But Vietnam defied the United States; China and Yugoslavia defied Moscow. Some say that no one will ever subject its enemy to a nuclear attack. But the United States did.

In short, this country now faces an unprecedented risk requiring unprecedented measures before new weapon deployments and developments make a U.S.–Soviet nuclear confrontation unavoidable. This is not a matter for partisan ploys or campaign posturing. Unless we are doomed to live—and die—in what General Omar Bradley called "a world of nuclear giants and ethical infants," we must get our national political house in order on this issue now.

*

Effectiveness in foreign affairs also requires rebuilding our economic strength, a task made more difficult by the annual diversion of enormous sums to nonproductive military weapons and facilities. But that task is made almost impossible by the lack of public confidence, the absence of any national consensus, and our inability to raise economic issues above the eddies and crosscurrents of partisan politics.

The most urgent economic task confronting the President and Congress is reduction of the federal budget deficit, now forecast to remain above an annual $200 billion level indefinitely. This country's national debt is scheduled to rise by as much in this decade as it did in the previous two hundred years of our history.

These deficits compete with private demand for capital, thereby curbing investment in the new technology and more productive facilities our competitive position requires, and driving up real interest rates and thus dollar exchange rates, with disastrous consequences for both our exports and our domestic competition with imports. Trying to rely principally on monetary remedies would only risk a renewal of inflation— and that would be equally harmful to our capital formation, productivity and exports.

The effect of these enormous deficits on investor

[ 37 ]

funds and confidence, on interest rates, housing, construction, and consumer installment purchases, and on export industries, also threatens to abort our current economic recovery and bring on still another downturn, resulting in still less taxable income, still more unemployed in need of aid, and still higher deficits.

Agreement on the need to cut the federal budget deficit is easy. But cutting the deficit, especially cutting it by the enormous amount required even to stabilize the national debt/gross national product ratio at its July 1983 level of 30 percent, requires two politically painful kinds of action—raising revenues and reducing expenditures. There are no politically painless shortcuts for either.

Little is left to eliminate from the Budget by way of assistance for the largely voteless poor. Only a small amount of revenue will result from higher taxes on the few who are very rich. Strong and continuing economic growth will not reduce the underlying structural imbalance between our revenue base and our spending commitments. Even a nuclear arms reduction treaty, particularly if accompanied by the strengthening of conventional forces necessary to avoid early reliance on nuclear arms, would hardly dent the defense budget. (Meanwhile, requesting new taxes to finance his resumption of the Cold War is as unappealing to President Reagan as it was to President Johnson to finance the Vietnam War.)

Which political party, which branch of government, which President, wants to be held responsible for raising tax rates for either individuals or corporations, or reducing tax credits, exemptions and deductions? It would be difficult to raise payroll taxes any higher. It would be self-defeating to tax savings at the expense of investment. But the present revenue base is too limited and full of holes to generate the funds needed to reduce these deficits.

Which political party, which branch of government, which President, wants to be held responsible for cutting expansion of or eligibility for the indexed middle-class entitlement programs like Social Security and Medicare, or the funds for repairing our crumbling infrastructure, or the pay or pensions of those who serve in our armed forces? If improving our international competitiveness requires an expansion in education and research or federal job retraining or business loans, what additional programs are to be cut to make room for them? How much can be cut from the defense budget while our NATO allies are still expected to increase their outlays, our armed services are expected to attract and retain quality personnel, and the Soviets are expected to recognize that they can never outgun us and should therefore negotiate reasonably?

The obvious answer is that neither political party, neither Congress nor the President, wants such responsibility. Pericles may have thought it "good judgment to accept odium in a great cause," but very few practicing politicians today are as politically secure as was Pericles. Nevertheless, the President and the Congress to be elected this year will not be able to evade this responsibility. The deficit will overwhelm us if it is not cut drastically in the next four years. "There is no way," says economist Alan Greenspan, "to resolve this issue without political pain."

*

In 1983, a comprehensive report by a task force of leading U.S. businessmen and educators declared that the restoration of this nation's ability to compete internationally should be our "central objective" for the rest of the decade.

> Other nations have . . . aggressive, coordinated strategies to meet the challenge of international competition. The United States has not. . . . We must develop a consensus that industrial competitiveness is crucial to our social and economic well-being.

There's that word again, consensus—so often sought, so rarely present. Yet the signs are increasingly evident that our economy is now passing through a period of traumatic transformation. Once our industry and labor force were supported almost exclusively by our own domestic market. Now, in the new era of transnational corporations, global communications, mobile capital, and instantaneous money and document transfers, they are increasingly competing in a single worldwide market.

The kind of mass-produced standardized item in which American industry led the world for so long is now turned out much more inexpensively in many parts of the Third World. In the race for international leadership in telecommunications, computer systems and other new industries, we may begin with superior strength in technology as well as capital, despite our declining support (as a percentage of gross national product) for science and research since the mid-sixties. But our position is adversely affected by our comparative rates of savings and investment, productivity, invention, interest and currency exchange.

In this increasingly interdependent world, we cannot solve our economic problems alone; nor can others prosper without us. Inflation and recession in America both feed and are fed by inflation and recession in the rest of the world. Our high interest rates draw capital away from our resentful industrial allies, weakening their currencies, increasing their borrowing rates, stifling their growth and increasing the pressures on them for protectionism. For the less developed countries, the combination of a stagnant American demand and excessive American interest rates spells hopeless debt, desperate poverty and new opportunities for demagogues and guerrillas. Although stopgap international financial first-aid treatment has thus far prevented a hemorrhage, their underlying trauma will remain until worldwide economic stagnation has ended.

A roller-coaster U.S. economy cannot compete with the rest of the world effectively. During the last decade, we have successively and sometimes simultaneously endured our lowest rate of growth since the Second World War; our highest rate of inflation, our longest recession and our highest rates of unemployment and bankruptcy and farm foreclosures in the same forty-year period; an unprecedented decline in our productivity, living standards and exports; our highest rates of interest, our highest peacetime federal budget deficits—and our highest level of political hypocrisy. For a decade and a half, we have been unable to achieve sustained growth without inflation, unable to end inflation without recession, and unable to reduce prices during recession. Each recession is deeper and longer than its predecessor and each interval between recessions grows shorter. The recovery which began in 1983 left in its wake unacceptably high unemployment, poverty and depression in several geographic and industrial sectors. Traditional fiscal and monetary doctrines have not solved any of the problems afflicting individual hard-hit sectors of the economy.

Confronting these issues is a politically painful task that neither party is eager to take on. What political leader, in this period of economic transition and readjustment, will explain to a worker in an aging industrial plant that protectionism will not prevent that worker's lifetime skills from being rendered obsolete by a single microchip performing one million operations per second? Who will change the popular tax and credit laws that encourage borrowing and consumption at the expense of U.S. savings accumulation and capital formation, which, as a percentage of gross national product, have declined to one of the lowest levels in the industrialized world? Who will accept the domestic political pressures involved in galvanizing the industrialized nations into harmonizing their economic, monetary, trade, credit, subsidy, exchange rate and development assistance policies?

These are not tasks that can be left to an independent Federal Reserve Board or delegated to a bipartisan Presidential commission. They will require all the elements in Washington that have been sadly lacking—confidence, consensus, Congressional-Executive cooperation, courageous statesmanship that rises above partisan politics—and speed. "In the international trade game," industrialist Lee Iacocca has observed, "time is not on our side. The next several seasons will determine, irreversibly, whether America stays in the world trade major leagues."

The next several years, in short, may bring irreversible moves toward a U.S.–Soviet nuclear confrontation or an irreversible decline in the strength of our economy. Time is running out.

# 3

## CHANGING COURSES,
## NOT MERELY HORSES

Oᴜʀ economic decline and nuclear destruction have
not become inevitable; our nation's problems have not
become unsolvable; our governmental affairs have not
become unmanageable. It is a tenet of our national religion, despite substantial historical evidence to the
contrary, that a kindly Providence looks out for fools,
babes and the United States of America, assuring the
emergence of a great leader in this country's time of
deepest crisis. Given the flaws and fissures in our political system today, that is asking a lot of the Almighty.

No doubt this year's crop of Presidential and Congressional candidates, campaign managers and committee members are confident that all problems can be
solved after this year's election. No doubt each candidate feels that winning control of the Presidency and
both houses of Congress by a large margin would ensure the political consensus and public confidence necessary for a newly effective White House to negotiate
successfully with the Soviets and to cut back the federal debt. That would surely be consistent with our

Constitutional theory that the public's periodic right to change the President or Congress after a spirited campaign enables the system to self-correct for any weakness.

Unfortunately, our political campaigns, as now constituted, have become part of the problem. Clearly, they do not assure a solution. Lyndon Johnson and Jimmy Carter enjoyed large Democratic majorities in the House and Senate after the 1964 and 1976 elections respectively, but their effectiveness in office steadily declined. Landslide victories for Nixon in 1972 and Reagan in 1980 did not remove for long the atmosphere of confrontation in Washington.

In each campaign, with each candidate, we are told it will be different. That much is true. Each election, like each candidate, is different. But the problems remain the same.

The very process of campaigning for the Presidency under the present system weakens the winner's ability to govern effectively. The special talents demanded by a Presidential campaign are for the most part not the skills needed in the White House. As Hedley Donovan, the journalist and Presidential adviser, has asked: "How did the machinery for identifying potential Presidents, nominating candidates and choosing winners come to be so seriously out of sync with the modern requirements of the office?"

Once there was a closer relationship between running and ruling. Twenty-four and more years ago, the qualities required to win the Presidential nomination and election resembled many of those required to govern the nation effectively. Those qualities included the political and ideological flexibility to woo and win over all kinds of political leaders, governors, mayors, party bosses and union presidents, as well as local precinct chairmen and grass-roots organizers; the sensitivity to understand and accept the separate political agenda of each; the ability to motivate and organize the countless volunteers needed in each locale; the discernment to make useful alliances and avoid needless enmities; the judgment to choose among potential policy positions and policy advisers with great care; the experience and intellect to know and understand thoroughly every nook and nuance of great national issues; the ability to articulate coherent national goals. The Presidential campaigns of the past tested those qualities and honed those skills as a useful prelude to the Presidency.

Today those qualities are still required for a President to govern effectively; but they have very little to do with success in the campaign.

Today working with governors, mayors and other concerned political leaders is far less important than getting the attention of millions of largely uninterested voters in nearly three dozen Presidential primaries.

Today choosing policy advisers is insignificant compared to lining up the right pollster, media adviser, direct mail operator, fund-raiser and makeup artist.

Today policy positions are not comprehensively articulated but condensed into bumper-sticker slogans and clever TV debate ripostes that will please everyone and offend no one.

Today experience and intellect are no more crucial to the multimedia campaign than the candidate's hair, teeth, smile and dog.

Today volunteers have been replaced by computerized mail, automated telephone banks and other marvels of technology in an industry that has shifted from labor intensive to capital intensive.

Today the news media rarely report what the candidates are saying on the issues. They report instead on a horse race—which horse is ahead, which one has the most physical stamina, which one is lame and which one is attracting the big money.

Money is the great equalizer in Presidential politics. Almost anyone, rich or poor, who can raise $15 million or $20 million can run for President. The total cost of this year's campaign for each of the major party candidates has been estimated at $60 million, up by more than one third from the 1980 total. Most of the estimated $20 million required for nomination comes not from the candidate's political party, with its familiar principles, accountability and continuity. Instead (except for federal matching funds) it is donated or raised by individuals and interest groups with their own special axes to grind, including corporate, labor union, trade association and ideological political action committees (PACs), and various lobbyists, lawyers, name-droppers, fixers and would-be ambassadors.

One reason for the cost is the ever-growing length of the American Presidential campaign. Each of the major candidates for the 1984 Democratic Presidential nomination was building his organization and war chest more than two years before the election. It is not surprising that politicians temporarily out of office— like Nixon, Carter and Reagan—have fared better in seeking the Presidential nomination than their rivals who had public duties to fulfill.

The excessive length of the modern Presidential campaign is sorely out of proportion to its intellectual depth. It is rarely the educational process that our political theory presupposes. In order to obtain money or support from organized interests, to make headlines in the press, to appear on the evening television news show, our candidates—often suppressing their previous positions or personal prudence—make unfulfillable promises to fit the exaggerated expectations of the moment. Like generals preparing to fight the last war, they debate the issues of the past and pledge to protect the entrenched status quo of their respective supporters, even as they orate about the future. Usually their statements are oversimplified to win the applause of each immediate audience. Not infrequently they are simply wrong—like John Kennedy decrying in 1960 a "missile gap" he later discovered to be nonexistent, or Ronald Reagan decrying in 1980 a "window of vulnerability" he was later told was never open. (No doubt, both were misinformed; but ignorance is a less acceptable excuse on the part of a candidate who is a President running for reelection.)

Foreign policy in particular suffers from campaign pressures. No powerful political constituency urges a Presidential candidate to help the developing nations or back the World Bank or strengthen the United Nations. But that candidate will continually encounter pressure groups strongly committed to a particular weapons systems or tariff increase or support for an ancestral homeland.

When self-interest is not involved, American public opinion on world affairs is too often uninformed, volatile or even sentimental, endowing foreign nations with the anthropomorphic characteristics of a particular leader whom we like or dislike from his photographs and headlines. Generally we prefer instant or dramatic solutions to the kind of steady, patient persistence required to build any lasting institutional arrangements. Long-drawn-out wars, long-drawn-out negotiations or long-drawn-out economic and political development efforts rarely remain popular in this country. As Lyndon Johnson, an avid consumer of opinion polls, once said: "What the American people like is action. . . . If I went to Hanoi to make peace, my popularity polls would immediately go up 10 percent—and they would be exactly the same if I bombed Peking. . . . [T]hey don't like . . . anything . . . measured."

In the same vein, an American military source, despairing of ever being given the time necessary to build a stable and enduring political center in El Salvador before that country is torn asunder by extremists, told the *New York Times* last year: "Americans like their wars quick, dirty and violent."

The natural temptation for a Presidential candidate is to cast blame for whatever is wrong on someone who has no vote to cast against him—blame the Japanese for increased unemployment, blame the Arabs for high fuel bills, blame the Russians for heavy defense costs. Blame the poor, who all too rarely vote, and the felons, who cannot vote. If no other target can be found, blame the opposition. Given the present hodgepodge dispersal of responsibility under our system, who can prove otherwise?

In short, regardless of whether one faults the parties, the public, the process or the Presidential candidates, it is doubtful that either party's conventional politics or political convention will produce this year an end to the cycle of political gridlock in Washington.

## STRUCTURAL REFORM

Could not this seriously flawed system for selecting the world's most important leader be improved? There is no shortage of suggested reforms: substituting a national primary, for example, or three or four regional primaries, extending public financing to Congressional campaigns, further limiting contributions to and by political action committees, requiring an earlier designation of party nominees (thereby making the real campaign even longer), realigning our two major political parties to produce one Liberal party and one Conservative party (forgetting that increasingly few politicians neatly fit either category on every issue), or returning to the era when the members of Congress had a more decisive role in the process (a practice ultimately resented and rejected by state and local party leaders). These and a long list of other suggestions deserve study. But they cannot be and should not be rushed through for 1984. On the contrary, any permanent structural changes in Presidential politics should be approached with great caution, in view of our unhappy experience with such reforms over the last decade and a half:

*Reform* 1: To reduce the power of political bosses and their ilk in national nominating conventions, binding primaries or open statewide caucuses were required in virtually every state. As a result, the candidates must now run some fifty separate television and direct mail campaigns, vastly elevating the importance to the candidate of money and media technique, and converting most national conventions into mere rituals of rhetoric, ratifying on the first ballot decisions already made at the state level by the small proportion of party members that votes in these primaries and caucuses.

*Reform* 2: To eliminate the scandalous spectacle of wealthy donors contributing enormous sums to future Presidents (and Congressmen), a federal campaign contribution limit of $1,000 per donor per election was enacted—without, however, reducing the total amount needed to compete nationwide. As a result, Presidential candidates—now required to raise their budgets from a far greater number of contributors—must devote a much larger part of their schedules, energies and staff to fund-raising events and to personal appeals to the wealthy.

*Reform* 3: To reduce still further the possibility of corruption in Presidential elections, public financing was provided to each major party nominee, with virtually all other contributions and expenditures prohibited. As a result, any state and local participation in the conduct of the Presidential campaign was virtually halted.

*Reform* 4: To open the nomination process to everyone, state delegate selection procedures were revised to encourage newcomers and to produce delegations that were proportionately representative as to race, area, age and gender. As a result, many of the party faithful and professionals—those who are expected to carry the party's water and tote the party's burdens year in and year out— were excluded from the process, replaced as delegates by followers of a single candidate, single issue or single organization, who may care very little about the party's traditions or long-range future.

*Reform* 5: To reduce the intolerable length of the campaign, Presidential primaries for 1984 were compressed into a shorter period. As a result, those candidates who previously hoped to emulate McGovern and Carter, by converting a surprisingly good showing in the early contests like Iowa and New Hampshire into a national campaign, were required this time to start raising big money and building a multistate organization long before election year arrived.

All these reforms were well intended. Together they have helped ensure that this country's system for selecting its head of government remains the most open system in the world, in which every candidate, regardless of fame or merit, has a chance to win, and every citizen, regardless of means or knowledge, has a chance to participate. But the blessings of democracy always exact a price; and we have paid a heavy price for these reforms in the additional handicaps and pressures imposed upon our Presidential candidates.

I take a similarly wary view of tinkering with the Constitution to solve our present deadlock—by limiting the President to a single six-year term, regardless of his ability and the nation's needs; by distributing portions of the President's power to the Cabinet or Congress, as though a less responsible President would be any better than an irresponsible President; or by merging executive and legislative powers as does the British parliamentary system, designed as it was for a smaller, less diverse country than ours with a more centralized government and political parties and a long-developed understanding of no-confidence votes and irregularly scheduled elections.

These proposals—even if meritorious or feasible— are capable neither of reforming our system in time to solve the problems now pressing upon us nor of addressing the *political* impasse that blocks those solutions. Permanent structural reforms cannot restore public confidence or consensus. As James MacGregor Burns wrote of similar suggestions to end what he called *The Deadlock of Democracy,* such proposals "have little bearing on the real problems of the President and Congress, which are problems not of misunderstanding or of faulty communication but of who gets what—and who does not."

Moreover, some advocates of structural change in our system have a disconcerting tendency to follow the election returns. When their own political leanings favor the party or policy of the White House incumbent, their learned analyses recommend permanent changes to strengthen the powers of the Presidency. When they oppose that incumbent, their analyses somehow result in recommendations for increased Congressional controls.

## TIME FOR A TRUCE

Our immediate need is not to make any permanent or fundamental alteration in the plan of those who framed our remarkable Constitution, but to save that plan through *voluntary* and *temporary* adjustments within that Constitutional framework. Unfortunately, in Walter Lippmann's words for an earlier day: "There are no precedents to guide us, no wisdom that wasn't made for a simpler age."

Stalemate and crisis also preceded the elections of 1860 and 1932. But each of those elections produced—as had seemed likely from the start of those respective campaigns—a clear-cut political mandate. This year's election now seems likely, regardless of the outcome, to perpetuate the existing political stalemate. That way lies a runaway arms race, a runaway deficit and, at a minimum, irreparable damage to this country's political and economic vitality.

Yet the next four years *could* be a period of progress and breakthrough—restoring our leadership as a champion of arms control, restoring our economic strength at home and abroad, restoring our confidence in our nation and system. To do that, we must create through compromise a national consensus that reaches beyond partisan politics.

Why not? If we strip away the ad hominem arguments, the disagreements on emphasis and tactics, and the extreme fringes in each party, there need be no exclusively "Republican answer" or "Democratic answer" to the basic questions of nuclear arms control, international competition, or even deficit reduction. These are problems more important than party labels. They require practical solutions not dependent upon ideology, personality or political history. Both parties share the blame for the plight in which we now find ourselves on these issues. Both must participate in reaching the necessary solutions, sharing whatever political pain comes with those solutions. Nothing else will work. Neither party can solve these problems alone. Neither can afford politically to stand in the way of a joint solution.

To paraphrase a David Lloyd George memorandum of 1910 urging a coalition, the built-in clash between the parties, and between the President and Congress, has served us well in the past and will again in the future; but the time has arrived for a truce.

Specifically, I believe the time has arrived in this country for a temporary bipartisan "grand coalition" of national unity. Its proposed operations and potential advantages are outlined in the remainder of this book. It would go beyond anything previously attempted or seriously considered in the United States. It would include, if adopted by the winner of the 1984 Presidential election, regardless of party:

- a President and Vice-President of opposite parties, each agreeing in advance to serve one term

only and to decline all partisan activities;
- a Cabinet and sub-Cabinet equally divided between the two parties;
- a small but experienced bipartisan White House staff acting as a unifying force in government;
- a Presidential Advisory Council of Elder Statesmen;
- a National Council of Economic Cooperation and Coordination, harmonizing the practices of private interests;
- a joint Executive-Congressional delegation to the U.S.–U.S.S.R. arms reduction talks; and
- a return to politics as usual at the end of four years.

Radical? Unprecedented? Maybe. Unworkable? Unacceptable? Maybe not. Unconstitutional? Incompatible with our system? Definitely not.

The American people have little faith today in either rigid ideology or narrow partisanship. The concept of one-party government is not engraved in the Constitution. On the contrary, *The Federalist Papers* made clear that parties were not needed or contemplated by the Framers; and our first President warned against them.

In a very real sense, the rudiments of a shaky de facto coalition government already exist in Washington today—half-formed, unofficial, tentative, inconsistent, unarticulated, and thus not successful, but an indication nevertheless of what may be both necessary and possible. Under the present grip of political gridlock, no important progress can be made except when clear agreement exists among the President and his advisers, both houses of Congress and both major political parties. There have been increased attempts at bipartisan bargains within Congress, increased resort to bipartisan appeals from former Cabinet members, and increased reliance on bipartisan commissions appointed by the President.

There have been calls for a "new unity" on foreign policy from a Republican Cabinet member (George Shultz), and calls for a bipartisan government to tackle economic problems from a potential Democratic Cabinet member (Felix Rohatyn). "For better or worse," says James Schlesinger, who served in both Republican and Democratic Cabinets, "we must master coalition politics." To devise the tax and budget measures necessary to slash the deficit, there have been calls from a Republican economist (Alan Greenspan) for a post-election "economic summit meeting" between the President and the Congressional leaders of both parties, and calls from a Democratic economist (Walter Heller) for a "bipartisan consensus and a growing atmosphere of compromise rather than confrontation." Horace Busby, in the lecture previously cited, foresaw public distaste for partisan excess leading to "the depoliticization of America."

An amorphous notion of reaching truly, not merely for show or expedience, beyond party lines is in the air in Washington. If it can be given a formal structure, officially established, organized on a continuing basis in the White House itself, and shielded from partisan exploitation, a bipartisan Coalition Government for one crucial four-year period could change, as was said of the Andrew Johnson Vice-Presidential nomination, "the destiny of the country itself."

It would be a new and daring experiment, and not all experiments succeed. It would demand a selfless and substantial sacrifice of power from the party victorious in November, and not all sacrifices prove worthwhile. This proposal is not risk-free.

But the chances of four unbroken years of effective progress on these critical deadlocked issues resulting in any other way—from bipartisan summits or commissions or calls for unity—are very slim. And continued deadlock is an unacceptable risk.

James Reston wrote early in 1983 about Republican and Democratic feuding: "One day maybe they'll get down to thinking about the future and the possibilities of cooperation between the parties. For if any one party ever does that, regardless of personalities, it may win the next election."

To stimulate that thinking about the future, to give some specific shape and substance to those possibilities of cooperation, is the purpose of this book.

# PART
# II

# A GRAND COALITION

# 4

## A COALITION CABINET

*In 1864, in the midst of a savage civil war, Abraham Lincoln, sixteenth President of the United States, launched his campaign for reelection with what Carl Sandburg called "a touch of the unreal, of a guess in twilight."*

*Despite deep and bitter protests about the draft, the war's continuing death toll, high taxes and inflation, Lincoln's own renomination by the "regular" Republican party was not in serious doubt. But he felt his reelection—and thus his goal of ending the secession and reconstituting the nation—was very much in doubt.*

*Lincoln had led the Republicans to their first Presidential victory in 1860 in a four-way electoral vote split in which he had received less than 40 percent of the popular vote. The Republicans were still a sectional party, a conglomeration of factions constantly in danger of coming apart. Of the eight Presidents to serve since Andrew Jackson, not one had been reelected, regardless of party. The effect on the voters of Lincoln's new Emancipation Proclamation was uncertain. In the early months of 1864, with casualties mounting at Olustee, Wilderness, Spotsylvania and Cold Harbor, and with Republican dissidents holding their own convention and nominating the once formidable John C. Frémont for President, Lincoln knew that "politics as usual" would not be enough to assure his reelection. Not with the Union hanging in the balance.*

*The Republican Convention, with Lincoln's blessing, was renamed the National Union Convention, with the hope that that label, and a platform suited to it, would draw outside support. But the Republican party's first President went further. He adroitly directed or permitted (historians differ) that "touch of the unreal"—the nomination by the convention of Andrew Johnson as his running mate, replacing the faithful Republican Vice-President of his first term, Hannibal Hamlin of Maine. Andrew Johnson was a Democrat.*

*He was not a nominal or fallen-away Democrat. He was a leading member of his party who had served as a Democratic Congressman, Governor and Senator from Tennessee, "the furnace of treason," and who had supported in 1860 Lincoln's Democratic opponent, John Breckenridge. "Can't you get a candidate for Vice-President," Thad Stevens reportedly complained, "without going down into a damned rebel province for one?"*

*Johnson did not leave the Democratic party to run for Vice-President as the Republican party's nominee. Instead, in his letter accepting the nomination, he publicly appealed to his "old friends of the Democratic Party proper":*

> *the hour has now come when that great party can justly vindicate its devotion to true Democratic policy. . . . [T]he path of duty is patriotism and principle. Minor considerations and questions of administrative policy should give way to the higher duty of first preserving the Government;*

and then there will be time enough to wrangle over the men and measures pertaining to its administration.

It was a strange political ticket, "a guess in twilight." Never before in American history had one of the two major parties nominated a prominent member of the opposition for Vice-President. The Twelfth Amendment to the Constitution had been expressly designed to alter the original provision by which a victorious President was required to accept as Vice-President his principal rival. Once political parties emerged in this country, harnessing Federalist President John Adams with Republican-Democrat Vice-President Thomas Jefferson proved uncomfortable and unworkable for all.

But Johnson, whom Lincoln had earlier appointed to be the Union's military governor of secessionist Tennessee, was in the President's eyes more than a Democrat. He was the ablest of the "War Democrats," a staunch opponent of secession, for which he had been hanged in effigy in Memphis. The nomination of this son of a poor tailor, Lincoln believed, offered to the country dramatic promise of an administration reaching beyond one section and one party. It offered to the British and French an urgently needed demonstration that the Union would be whole again and that diplomatic recognition of the Confederacy would be a mistake. As one of Lincoln's agents at the convention explained, the selection of Johnson "involved the destiny of the country itself."

The experiment worked. Lincoln won overwhelmingly, carrying border states like Maryland and Missouri, which he had lost in 1860. His second term was, tragically, cut short, but he had fulfilled his hopes for a victory and an *administration that reached beyond a single section and party.\**

IF this country is to achieve a bipartisan consensus on the most critical issues now confronting us, it is not enough for a President or candidate to pledge that he will be "a President of all the people, regardless of party," dedicated to serving the interests and meeting the needs of every citizen. Virtually every President makes that pledge. Even while making it, he is actively favoring his party in appointments and other benefits and acting as his party's chief strategist, fund-raiser and cheerleader.

It is not enough for a President or candidate to call for a bipartisan foreign policy or for a nonpartisan approach to key issues. Virtually every President makes that call—at least when it is expedient, particularly when he is uncertain of Congressional or public support. But then he goes his own way whenever he can, particularly if he and his party get more political benefit from not sharing the spotlight with the opposition.

It is not enough for a Presidential candidate to pledge that he will appoint to his Cabinet "the ablest people in the country, regardless of party." Virtually every Presidential candidate makes that pledge. The usual result is still a Cabinet composed almost entirely of his party's followers.

*Even before his moderate course as Lincoln's successor antagonized the radical Republicans during Reconstruction, leading to his impeachment and near conviction, Johnson had impaired his reputation by an inane and apparently inebriated speech at the Inauguration. But in the brief period they served together, Lincoln consulted with him regularly, remarking to a friend, "He is too much of a man for the American people to cast him off for a single error."

It is not enough that a President place in his Cabinet, as a demonstration of bipartisanship, individuals who were once registered in or even prominently identified with the opposition party but who are now better known for their strong disagreement with that opposition party and their support of the new President (like Franklin Roosevelt bringing in Henry Wallace and Harold Ickes as domestic policy Republicans, or Ronald Reagan bringing in Jeane Kirkpatrick as a foreign policy Democrat).

What is required is the creation of a truly bipartisan administration, including the selection of a Vice-President from the opposition party and the appointment of a Coalition Cabinet composed of outstanding men and women from the active ranks of each of the two major parties, half from each. Although most of them would undoubtedly come from the more moderate wing of their respective parties, it is important that those appointed to represent the opposition not be so far removed from that party's mainstream and favor as to be wholly unrepresentative. (Obviously, their ranks must not be confined to those who openly supported the new President.) Within the Cabinet and National Security Council, the key posts should also be equally divided. Each Cabinet member's number one deputy or under secretary should be an active member of the party to which that Cabinet member does not belong.

Cabinet members—individually, in small groups and as a body—must be given greater participation in the formulation of administration policy than they have been given by most modern Presidents, with their aggressive White House staffs. (As noted in the next chapter, the role and composition of the Coalition White House staff will also depart sharply from recent practice.) The Coalition President and Vice-President should agree on the composition of the Cabinet and the selection of such non-Cabinet appointees as Chairman of the Joint Chiefs of Staff, Chairman of the Federal Reserve Board and Director of Central Intelligence.

The first crucial test of a Presidential candidate's sincere commitment to genuine Coalition Government—the first real signal of his intention to pay more than lip service to the concept—would come with his first important Cabinet "appointment": namely, his selection of a Vice-President from the other party. The timing of this signal, and thus the timing of his open support for and implementation of a Coalition approach, would depend upon his assessment of the following four options:

- First, in the spring of this election year, as a *candidate* for the Presidential nomination, he could declare in a campaign speech or press conference that he intends to form a Coalition Government and will therefore select a Vice-Presidential running mate from the other major party. The candidate adopting this approach would surely capture the attention of those Presidential primary and caucus voters looking for a leader who can end the morass in Washington. But he would also be required to forgo the traditional political device of dangling a possible Vice-Presidential nomination in front of several party leaders whose support he needs for the nomination. In addition, he would risk the resentment of party leaders more interested in the joys of partisan battle or the spoils of Presidential patronage than in the need for bipartisan progress.

• Second, at his party convention, as the party's Presidential *nominee,* he could appear before the assembled party delegates, outline the need for a Coalition Government and, invoking the Presidential nominee's traditional right to select his own running mate, designate the talented man or woman from the other major party whom he wished the convention to nominate for Vice-President. The majority of convention delegates, having given him the Presidential nomination, would be most unlikely to refuse this request, however angry or astonished some leaders might be. Revealing his commitment to Coalition at this stage could not risk his nomination and might well have sufficient public appeal to enhance his prospects for election. (Should both major party nominees see merit in this bipartisan approach, that remarkable turn of events would not diminish the importance of each voter's choice. The abilities and views of the two nominees would almost surely not be identical; their commitments to lead a genuinely bipartisan effort are unlikely to be perceived as equally credible; and even in a coalition of compromise, the direction of the public's mandate and the qualities of leadership in the top two positions would be crucial. Who wins would still matter. But a contest between two mixed-party tickets would certainly be different!)

- Third, after the election, as *President-elect*, he could announce an agreement with his Vice-President-elect (a member of his own party) on the latter's having been selected for a Cabinet or other high post, and then ask all Electoral College members to choose as his new Vice-President the individual whom he had selected from the opposition party. Public opinion surveys have repeatedly concluded that American voters do not base their vote for a Presidential candidate on the identity of his Vice-Presidential running mate, much less on the expectation that the individual so chosen will greatly influence the President. For that reason, particularly if the Vice-President-elect remains in the new Administration in a position of authority, no one will be able to argue successfully that this arrangement constitutes a trick or fraud upon the electorate. Nevertheless, the Presidential candidate contemplating this move would be better off revealing his intentions before the election, even if he does not then identify his future Vice-President. In either event, confronted with a vacancy in the Vice-President-elect position, and free under the Constitution to exercise their individual discretion, the majority of electors, meeting in those states carried by the President-elect, would surely be responsive to his wishes. It is even possible that the Vice-Presidential substitute whom he puts forward, a leader of the opposition party, would receive ballots from some of the Electoral College members of that party, who are also theoretically free to exercise their discretion. Instead of going through the motions of recording their votes for the Vice-Presidential nominee on the losing ticket, they might well feel that the voters whom they represent would approve of their using this opportunity to show their party's bipartisan spirit as well as the opportunity to cast a more meaningful ballot for a fellow party member. Were that to occur, the new Coalition would take office with at least some show of formal support under the Constitution from more than one party. (It is always possible that the leader from the other party to be selected as the substitute Vice-President would be the defeated opposition candidate for Vice-President—or even the defeated candidate for President, though he would probably be a less comfortable harness mate.) By delaying his ultimate choice of a Vice-President until after the election, the President could better judge who would best heal the wounds created by the campaign.

Finally, upon his inauguration as *President*, perhaps as part of his "unity" Inaugural Address, he could announce a similar agreement with the Vice-President (on the latter's being slated for a new post) and send to Congress the nomination of a new Vice-President from the ranks of the opposition party, such nomination to be confirmed under the Twenty-fifth Amendment by a majority vote in both houses. By Inauguration time, of course, identification of the bipartisan members

[ 69 ]

of the President's new Coalition Cabinet would have made clear the unusual nature and direction of the new administration. Senate confirmation of those new Cabinet and other nominees, as discussed below, would present an important opportunity to demonstrate Executive-Legislative harmony. But by choosing the one Vice-Presidential selection option of these four that requires the participation of both houses of Congress in the confirmation process, the new President could offer symbolic evidence of his new Coalition Government's intention to assure full Congressional involvement in all key decisions. Sending to the Senate the nomination of the originally elected Vice-President to serve in a different but responsible Administration post would also be consistent with a unity approach. Precedent of a sort exists in Franklin Roosevelt's decision, possibly influenced in part by the limited bipartisan atmosphere of the 1944 election, to shift Vice-President Henry Wallace back to the Cabinet and take a new running mate, Harry Truman. (Nor is it unprecedented for a Vice-President to resign without dishonor, John C. Calhoun having done so when elected to the United States Senate in 1832.)

In short, each of these four options has advantages and disadvantages to be weighed by the would-be Coalition President in the context of his prospects for nomination, election and effective governance. He might find it impolitic or impractical to disclose such a plan before his nomination or to implement it before his election. He might well find it impossible, until after he is elected, to obtain the right Vice-President from the other party—a man or woman who is not only capable of running the country upon the death or permanent disability of the President, but also genuinely representative of the other party. That individual may prefer to support his or her party's own ticket in November and accept this unusual offer only after it is clear that doing so can no longer harm that ticket's chance to win the White House this year.

Not everyone would accept; not just anyone should be asked. The President and Vice-President in a Coalition of the kind of envisaged must share, from their separate perspectives, a common understanding of the nation's current stalemate and a common willingness to accept the compromises necessary to break it. The President must be willing to give to the Vice-President a larger role than any previous occupant of that office has assumed, including participation in all key meetings and decisions.

Concepts like coalition, consensus and compromise would not appeal to rigid ideologues. Nor could those political leaders who are perceived, fairly or unfairly, as extreme partisans successfully fill either spot on a Coalition ticket. The spirit of consensus can work wonders but not miracles. The lion and the lamb will not lie down together—at least not this year.

I do not expect the concept of bipartisan Coalition to be adopted or credibly offered by any candidate for the Presidency whose record to date has been widely perceived by the opposition as outside the mainstream.

Nor would I expect anyone so perceived to be offered the Vice-Presidential position on a Coalition ticket. I do not expect to see the Democrats nominate a Coalition ticket of Jerry Brown and Jerry Falwell, for example, or the Republicans a ticket of Jesse Helms and Jesse Jackson.

But a Coalition ticket need not be confined to those with identical views. Within their respective parties, Franklin Roosevelt, John Kennedy and Ronald Reagan all chose running mates with whom they had stoutly debated and differed. Each of those teams worked in harmony without either the President or the Vice-President totally suppressing his individual principles.

Democrat Andrew Johnson agreed to run and work with Republican Abraham Lincoln in the belief that this kind of unity in wartime was best for both country and party. Surely, in this critical election year, particularly as part of a full-scale Coalition Government (which Lincoln did not offer Johnson), any number of prominent and experienced men and women in each of our two major parties should be willing, if asked, to accept the Vice-Presidency on the opposition team. They would accept in the same spirit of public service and national interest as Republican Douglas Dillon displayed in serving in the administrations of Presidents Eisenhower and Kennedy, and as Democrat Daniel Patrick Moynihan displayed in serving in the administrations of Presidents Kennedy and Nixon. Henry Stimson, in Roosevelt's war Cabinet, described himself as a "Republican doing non-partisan work for a Democratic President because it related to international affairs in which I agreed and sympathized with all his policies."

Men and women willing to accept that same approach could surely be found for every position in a Coalition Cabinet, as well as the Vice-Presidency. If, in the course of the past two years, six former Secretaries of the Treasury, five former Secretaries of Commerce and ten other former Cabinet members, from both parties, could agree on how to reduce the Budget deficit, six former Secretaries of Labor from both parties could agree on the scope of a federally financed jobs program, eight former Secretaries of Health and Human Services from both parties could agree on a national welfare proposal, six former Secretaries of State from both parties could agree on the United States contribution to the International Monetary Fund, and four former Commissioners of Education from both parties could agree on new federal education initiatives, then surely it should be possible for a new Coalition President to find for each Cabinet and sub-Cabinet position distinguished men and women from both parties who would be willing to subordinate partisan considerations and to compromise personal views in order to serve the national interest in a bipartisan coalition— and make it work.

The great majority of those most likely to be interested in serving in a Coalition Cabinet, and the great majority of those most likely to be asked, would necessarily come (like the potential Coalition Vice-President) from the ranks of those Republicans and Democrats perceived as more moderate and less extreme. That would not be unrepresentative of an American electorate that has largely though not exclusively looked to the middle. Over the years, major party

[ 73 ]

nominees like Barry Goldwater and George McGovern received comparatively few electoral votes; and third-party nominees like Strom Thurmond, George Wallace and Henry Wallace received few or none at all.

Any President's Cabinet choices are among the most important and difficult decisions he will make. Well-known figures are rarely equal to their reputations. Those whom the President does not know will often seem to have fewer faults than those whose limitations he knows through personal acquaintance. Frequently a President will choose as the head of each department an individual who specializes in the subjects handled by that department and is likely to be of little help in other areas—not a suitable choice for a Coalition Cabinet. Most Presidents tend to overlook talent already in the Executive Branch. Appointing former longtime members of Congress (or sitting members willing to resign), if they have the respect of their former colleagues, can help bridge the checks-and-balances gap. (Only Eisenhower of all the twentieth-century Presidents failed to appoint at least one Cabinet member who had been elected to Congress.)

Searching primarily for experienced leaders, unrestricted in that search, as never before, by party labels and lists of campaign contributors, a Coalition President—in a position to offer a prospective nominee at least some diminution of the usual partisan fire from Congress—should be able to recruit and retain men and women of unusual ability and background who might not otherwise be interested. No nominee will or should escape all scrutiny and criticism; but a group of dedicated and experienced men and women willing to go in, take four years of pressure and get out would reduce this country's distressingly high rate of Cabinet and sub-Cabinet turnover. That in turn would reduce the time now spent by new and inexperienced appointees in on-the-job training, and possibly reduce the press and Congressional suspicions often visited upon newer, less familiar and possibly more ambitious nominees.

To be sure, American history offers little precedent for a President appointing to his Cabinet and successfully working with prominent, active believers from the opposition party. Democratic (then called Republican) party founder Jefferson served with Hamilton, Adams and other emerging Federalists in George Washington's originally nonpartisan Cabinet. But he ultimately resigned from that Cabinet; and Washington later said: "I shall not, while I have the honor to administer the government, bring a man into an office of consequence knowingly, whose political tenets are adverse to the measures which the general government is pursuing; for this in my opinion would be a sort of political suicide."

When Jefferson later became the first President to take office after a change in party control, he expressed noble bipartisan sentiments in his Inaugural Address: "We are all Republicans, we are all Federalists." But he kept no Federalists in his Cabinet.

James Monroe may have proclaimed and enjoyed a nonpartisan "era of good feeling," carrying every state in his bid for reelection; but his own good feeling did not extend to including anyone from the dying Federalist party in his Cabinet.

Military hero Zachary Taylor won the Presidency in 1849, it was said, because he had no party—and no policies, principles, enemies or political stature; but once elected, he was enough of a Whig not to appoint any Democrats to the Cabinet.

Soon after this country became involved in the First World War, a bipartisan "War Cabinet," to be led by former Republican President Theodore Roosevelt, was urged upon Democratic President Woodrow Wilson as necessary for military effectiveness and as a mate to Britain's wartime coalition. But Wilson was unwilling to listen to any such scheme (much less to Theodore Roosevelt).

Eisenhower, less of a partisan Republican before his Presidency than after, appointed union leader and Democrat Martin Durkin to a Cabinet otherwise composed of wealthy Republicans. But Durkin was soon out.

In contrast to this discouraging history, Republicans like Henry Stimson, Frank Knox, Robert Lovett, John McCloy, Paul Hoffman, Arthur Dean and John Foster Dulles all performed distinguished service for Democratic Presidents during the Second World War and in the establishment of NATO, the Marshall Plan, Greek-Turkish aid, the reconstruction of West Germany and Japan, and a free and economically revived Western Europe. Had Woodrow Wilson similarly involved the Republican opposition in the shaping of this country's policy after the First World War, history might have been different.

It was said of Democrat John Kennedy's Cabinet that, in contrast with most, it contained only one large campaign contributor—Republican Douglas Dillon, who had contributed over $26,000 to Kennedy's Republican opponent. Kennedy's Secretary of Defense and National Security Adviser also had Republican backgrounds, as did a host of outside and part-time advisers.

Moreover, some of the strongest Presidential Cabinets in our history—including those of Jefferson and Lincoln—though limited largely if not exclusively to members of the President's own party, contained individuals with political interests, ambitions and views sharply at variance with those of the President who appointed them: past and future Presidential rivals, factional party leaders, statesmen whose fame exceeded that of the President himself. But they could still work effectively as a team.

James Buchanan advised President-elect Franklin Pierce to avoid placing such factional powerhouses in his Cabinet, or he would "discover that he has only infused into those factions new vigor and power for mischief." Pierce took this advice and succeeded in creating the only Cabinet in American history that required no changes throughout the President's term— and one of the weakest Cabinets in American history.

Contrast that with Churchill's effective coalition cabinet in Britain during the Second World War—in a country that, in Disraeli's phrase, does not love a coalition. France, Jean Daniel has written, had a successful coalition cabinet, a "Sacred Union" of all political factions, under Clemenceau during the First World War and de Gaulle after the Second World War because "exceptional circumstances justified exceptional measures and allowed them to move beyond ideology."

To be sure, successful foreign coalitions—involving a system of cabinet government, parliamentary rule and often too many political parties to permit any one party to gain and maintain a majority—offer no assurance of success under our very different system and tradition. More important, foreign coalitions have failed more often than they have succeeded. They are rarely as long-lasting or productive as their founders hoped. A falling-out or internal deadlock between coalition members, or public dissatisfaction with the results of constant compromising on Cabinet appointments or policies, can undermine the most solemn vows of cooperation. Even in those countries where emergency coalitions were successful, the voters have usually gone promptly and enthusiastically back to partisan politics as soon as the emergency ended. Witness, for example, Britain's ousting of Churchill in 1945.

But coalition government in a democracy should be temporary. Two-party politics should return and inevitably will return. A similar theme can be found in our own political history, replete as it is with examples of one-party landslides followed four years later by razor-thin margins, and examples of solidly one-party states becoming hotly contested two-party states. Most assuredly, the proposal contained in this book contemplates no more than a four-year limited truce between the parties.

Even during that truce, the parties would not disappear. Politics and political opposition would not disappear. Government is politics and politics includes compromise. The President, Vice-President and Cabinet would still need all their political skills to formulate, agree upon and win Congressional and public support for a workable program. They would still govern only with the consent of the governed, building a consensus for what is reasonable, rejecting the unrealistic and unacceptable. That is politics. They would still be accountable for their deeds and mistakes to the Congress, the courts, the public and the public's surrogate, the press.

A Coalition of moderates from both parties would still be confronted with opposition, criticism and alternative solutions from politicians at either end of the spectrum. Political debate, dissent and choice would remain very much alive. Each party in the Coalition, even while collaborating with the other side, would fulfill Jefferson's definition of the basic function of party divisions: "to induce each to watch, and relate to the people, the proceeding of the other."

Each of the two major parties would be tested severely if and when such a Coalition could be put together. The party victorious in this year's Presidential election would be submerging its natural desire for total executive power and patronage. The party defeated in the election would be submerging its natural desire to draw the line on every Administration appointment and proposal that offered an opportunity to win votes in the next round. In each party, those who felt they were not represented in the moderate Coalition would argue that the party's very existence and reason for existence were threatened, that traditional supporters would be alienated and traditional principles abandoned.

But in times as critical as these, I believe the voters will welcome the sight of Republicans and Democrats working together. The two major parties in this country, less divided by distinctions of social class, occupation and religion than the major parties in most democracies, may even find temporary Coalition easier than our foreign friends and allies have found it. Our Presidents have more than once adopted basic planks from the national convention platform of the opposition. Our opposition parties rarely put forward, as agreed-upon party positions, full-scale alternatives to Administration proposals. Any decline as a result of Coalition in the American public's present opportunity to hear the merits of two sharply contrasting programs would be minimal.

The members of the Coalition Cabinet, while refraining from attacking each other in public, can be expected to engage in vigorous private debate, debate that would be noted less for its rhetoric than for its quiet reasoning. Consensus does not mean diluting every controversy to the point of insignificance, dividing every issue down the middle, reducing every policy to the lowest common denominator. Nor does unity require unanimity, pleasing every faction and reflecting every view. We have had Presidents who lacked a basic philosophy of their own, who tried to appeal to every voter and to fudge every issue, with results as bad as those produced by ideological inflexibility.

A Coalition Government can be truly bipartisan, with input from both sides, and still have a basic direction and philosophy of its own. It will almost by definition be a centrist, moderate and flexible philosophy: in domestic policy, basically in tune with our longtime mix of private enterprise and public standards, open to progressive change in our system but not radical reconstruction, unwilling to leave the fate of either individuals or the economy to the vicissitudes of the marketplace but cognizant of the need to reduce public expenditures, neither anti-labor nor anti-business as it seeks the confidence and cooperation of both; and in foreign policy, neither isolationist nor confrontational, unwilling to rely wholly on either arms or diplomacy, and responding to Soviet power with neither unilateral disarmament nor obsessive intransigence. The purists in both parties will be uncomfortable watching this process of consensus-building; but the practical politicians both inside and outside the Cabinet should feel very much at home.

If the President can give each party and factional leader participating in the Coalition Cabinet a share and a stake in that Coalition's decisions, if each of them in turn can undertake to enlist—in support of those decisions—his allies in the Congress and general public, then this country may well, for the first time in two decades, experience four continuous years of decisive, effective government. A new consensus on crucial foreign and domestic issues can be shaped through the reconciliation of competing interests and the acceptance of constructive compromise. Public confidence in those policies and in our governmental processes can be restored.

It will not be easy. A temporary change in procedures and institutions will not by itself solve deep-seated substantive issues that were not created solely by procedural or institutional inadequacies. A Coalition might only weaken the Presidency, add new layers of advice and dissent, increase the divisions and delays in government, and raise still higher the barriers to change. But the alternative is perpetuation of the status quo—relying on bipartisan appeals, bipartisan summits and bipartisan commissions without the actual bipartisan sharing of power, risk, benefit and blame that is needed to assure success.

America's first Coalition Cabinet will be an unprecedented, uncharted and hazardous experiment. But in the words of de Tocqueville: "A democracy can obtain truth only as the result of experience."

# 5

# A ONE-TIME ONE-TERMER

*In 1958, the two traditional political parties of the South American nation of Colombia, the Conservative and the Liberal, concluded a unique bargain. Having regained their country from dictatorship only to confront economic despair, internal violence and the threat of a new uprising or strongman, they agreed upon an unprecedented sixteen-year National Front Coalition. Every four years, for sixteen years, the Presidency was to be alternated between the two parties. Each of those four Presidential Cabinets, and all sub-Cabinet appointments, were to be divided equally between the two parties. Lower-level officials were for the first time to be selected solely on the basis of merit. The Congress was to defer more often to the coalesced Executive.*

*Partisan politics can be fierce in Colombia. Neither party under normal circumstances would willingly surrender the Presidency after only one four-year term. But both parties adhered to this bargain for sixteen years (and in some respects longer). Not all the features of the Colombian National Front Coalition could be or should be emulated in other countries. Nor can it be said to have pro-*

*duced any dramatic breakthroughs for Colombia. But neither did it permit any drastic breakdowns. Domestic violence was contained. Economic development did go forward. Moderate and professionally developed policies were adopted. The Colombia Coalition was a success.*

*By each party refraining—for that limited period— from its insistence that the country go its way or no way at all, by each party submitting to cooperation and compromise for a fixed number of years before resuming its normal ambition, the country was saved from new disaster. As former President Alberto Lleras Camargo said, the coalition's purpose was "to do everything that the two parties had said should be done, but that each had not allowed the other to do." Losing the Presidency after four years in power was better than losing the country.*

THE burden and the glory of leading the Coalition Cabinet and the United States of America during the next four years, should the course of Coalition be selected, will fall upon the person elected as President in November of this year. More than most Presidents, he will rely upon his Cabinet members for advice and assistance, shaping with them the consensus that he hopes to build with their help in the Congress and the country. But our Constitutional system will still place upon the only leader elected by the entire nation the responsibility for final decisions. He cannot legally or justly be outvoted by an unelected Cabinet. The Framers of our Constitution deliberately departed from the provisions of most state constitutions of that time in rejecting the establishment of an executive council whose approval the President required.

[ 84 ]

Effective action will still require effective leadership. Group decisions from a Coalition Cabinet and bipartisan bargains with the Congress will still require one person with the legal and personal authority, strength, imagination and determination to envision and articulate and push and shape and pull together the basic effort that the Coalition hopes to accomplish. The Coalition President will be no more able to "control" Congress or the political opposition than his predecessors were. The leadership skills required to mold a consensus are very different—and in some ways more demanding—than those required in a confrontation. Patience, tact, diplomacy, restraint, and a capacity to distinguish between substance and verbiage and between priorities and subsidiary issues are among the qualities needed. The consensus-building President will be less dogmatic, less egocentric and less rigid than some of his predecessors; but he will be no less the leader of the government and nation.

Under those circumstances, the President in a Coalition Administration must be perceived by the Cabinet, the Congress and the nation as acting without partisan motives. He must relinquish the traditional Presidential role of party leader. He must abolish the traditional White House staff position overseeing party activities. He must renounce the traditional Presidential prerogative of selecting and replacing his party's National Chairman. He must avoid the party fundraising dinner circuit. He must refuse to make partisan campaign speeches, either in midterm or at term's end, either *for* any member of his party who has not wholeheartedly supported the Coalition or *against* any member of the opposition party who has wholeheartedly supported the Coalition. He must, in his press conferences and speeches, avoid any partisan claims or attacks. Most important, he must prove his good-faith commitment to bipartisan coalition by declaring from the start that he will not be a candidate for reelection in 1988.*

The Vice-President under the Coalition, who could at any moment succeed the President even though a member of the other party, should publicly commit himself to abide by all of these same constraints.

Should acceptance of the Coalition approach be declared at the outset of this year's campaign, then both the Presidential candidate adopting this course and his Vice-Presidential running mate would need to adopt similar guidelines even before the 1984 election. (This would not affect fund-raising for the national ticket's expenditures, inasmuch as funds for both parties now come almost exclusively from the federal Treasury.) It is possible that, in the midterm election, the Coalition President and Vice-President could go still further and make campaign appearances in support of Congressmen who are not members of their respective parties but who had faithfully supported the Coalition's legislative program.

A voluntary commitment not to seek a second term would be both a major sacrifice and a major departure from precedent. Since Rutherford B. Hayes, every incumbent President who survived his first full or inherited term in the White House has sought another four

* Should Ronald Reagan be reelected President, of course, he could not Constitutionally seek a third term in 1988 in any event.

years; and since Chester Alan Arthur, no incumbent President seeking the Presidential nomination has failed to receive it from his party's convention. The Democrats in 1980 were the first political party in this century to lose Executive Branch responsibility in Washington only four years after regaining it. Both personal and party ambitions will weigh heavily against a no-second-term announcement.

But history does not weigh in totally on the negative side of the scale. Three nineteenth-century Presidents—Polk, Buchanan and Hayes—chose not to seek a second term. In this century, Theodore Roosevelt, Calvin Coolidge, Harry Truman and Lyndon Johnson, each having served less than eight years (each having become President upon the death of his predecessor and then having won election in his own right), chose not to run for the second full term that neither law nor tradition prohibited.

The voluntary departure of an incumbent President at the end of his term has not assured either failure or success for his party in the next Presidential election (Republican Presidents did follow the voluntary departures of Republicans T. Roosevelt and Coolidge; Democratic Presidents did not follow the voluntary departures of Democrats Truman and Johnson). But neither does a one-term President striving to be returned to the White House have any assurance that he will not lose (as happened in this century to Taft, Hoover, Ford and Carter, all after only one term). Of President Reagan's fourteen predecessors in this century, only four enjoyed more than one Presidential election victory. No shame would be attached to a Coalition President's departing undefeated after four years.

In any event, the voluntary one-term limitation on this President is essential to the Coalition's prospects for success. A Presidential candidate cannot credibly propose more than four years of Coalition—an untried, unprecedented, but necessary experiment, a unique departure from our tradition of adversary politics. (If by 1988 Coalition has proved successful but requires more time, new candidates from one or both parties could then propose its extension.) He cannot credibly propose less than four years of Coalition, with his administration reverting to partisanship in the middle of his term; and in that same vein, he cannot credibly suggest that his own tenure as President might extend beyond the four-year life of the Coalition, into a new round of partisan politics.

An atmosphere of genuine bipartisanship requires both an absence of Presidential sniping at the opposition and vice versa. As the events of the last twelve months have made clear, a President can neither effectively call for nor legitimately expect an end to partisan attacks on his policies when he is a candidate or even a potential candidate for reelection. A Coalition President could not ask the opposition members of his Cabinet to help build the platform on which he intended to seek reelection as a partisan. Renouncing the right to seek reelection will not immunize the President and his program from opposition attack; but a program and Cabinet perceived as truly bipartisan are sure to receive relatively less hostile partisan fire. Thus the two key concepts—a bipartisan team and a one-term Presidency—reinforce each other in temporarily reducing the politicization of our national government.

Politics in its best and broadest sense will not be and should not be wholly absent, as indicated in the previous chapter. This country does not want an apolitical President, neither a "man on a white horse" who proclaims himself to be above politics nor a mere national administrator who is indifferent to voter concerns. I agree with Harry Truman: "A politician is a man who understands government, and it takes a politician to run a government." Even a one-term President, accountable to Congress and the courts, limited by the cooperation of the bureaucracy, concerned about the judgments of public opinion and history, rising to the Oval Office from a political background and base that he can never wholly abandon, will be practicing every day the art of politics in its highest form.

Once the Congress, public and bureaucracy know that he will not be President again, will they be less willing to cooperate, rendering him an ineffective "lame duck"? The only full Presidential term in our history known from the start to be the incumbent's last four years in the White House was the second term of Dwight D. Eisenhower. The first President to be affected by the Twenty-second Amendment to our Constitution, banning a Presidential third term, "Ike," in the view of both contemporary politicians and historians, was no crippled waterfowl from January 1957 until January 1961. Even though the opposition party controlled both houses of Congress, his second term was no less effective than his first. After all, his power under the Constitution to conduct foreign affairs, to initiate legislation, to formulate the Budget, to control appointments, to award patronage, to bestow favors and to appeal to the public was undiminished—as it would be for a one-term Coalition President. His policies had the same political basis and public appeal as ever. If anything, his ability to reach beyond his party was enhanced by the knowledge that he was not speaking as a potential candidate for reelection.

Should we therefore adopt the proposed Constitutional amendment that would limit every President to a single six-year term? No—and not only because six years is too long for a bad President. Under normal conditions, a successful President is right to seek a second four-year term. It is also right that he then be subjected, under our system of adversary politics—which is apparently deplored by some supporters of this proposed Constitutional amendment—to a healthy and democratic referendum on his performance. The very limited pool of extraordinary men and women able to make a success of the Oval Office should not be further limited by a permanent ban on those who know most about that Office. (In short, even though eight years will ordinarily exhaust a President's physical, intellectual and political resources, Washington and Hamilton were right in opposing a ban on third terms, and the Twenty-second Amendment was wrongfully conceived.)

Encouraging one President to limit his tenure voluntarily under unique and temporary circumstances, as proposed here, risks far less damage to our system than forcing every future President to limit his tenure regardless of circumstances, as the proposed Constitutional amendment would provide. The leader of a bi-partisan Coalition Government, peculiarly dependent upon the trust and confidence of the opposition party for his success, would pose far fewer dangers of unac-countability than would the new leader of the usual one-party administration who under the proposed amendment would assume the enormous powers of that office knowing from his first day onward that he is in effect no longer dependent on the consent of the governed.

A President committed to a one-time, four-year ex-periment in bipartisan Coalition as a means of breaking the current political deadlock on urgent issues, and wise enough to know that he could never maintain bi-partisan support in that Coalition were he to become a candidate for reelection on his party's ticket—a Presi-dent, moreover, who has demonstrated both the self-confidence and the dedication required to waive vol-untarily his right to seek a second term—will surely be perceived by Congress and the bureaucracy in a more positive light than a President denied that right by forces not of his making.

Even Washington in his Farewell Address took some satisfaction from the *voluntary* nature of his de-parture from the political scene. When Lyndon John-son decided to waive his right to seek reelection in 1968—according to the testimony of his Secretary of Defense, Clark Clifford—LBJ's legislative program benefited from the lingering suspicion in Congress that he might be persuaded to change his mind. Washing-ton would not have had that sense of satisfaction, or

Johnson that continuing power, had their departures been Constitutionally mandated instead of initiated by their own free will.

But my opposition to a permanent Constitutional ban on any President's right to run for reelection does not blind me to the advantages of a one-time Coalition President's willing surrender of that right. Far more than a President seeking reelection, he will be able to separate, in his mind and his speeches, the long-range public interest from short-term public opinion. Long ago, Lord Bryce reported that he found in this country too many a politician—not only in the White House—who was "always listening for the popular voice, always afraid to commit himself to a view which may turn out to be unpopular" and thus unable to "penetrate beneath the superficialities of the newspaper and the platform." Those limitations are not wholly escapable in a democracy; but they will be minimized in a bipartisan Coalition Government, particularly when the President is not seeking reelection.

There will be no temptation to postpone difficult questions until after the election (as Ford did on the Panama Canal in 1976 and Carter did on SALT II in 1980), no reckless reach for a "quick fix" (like Johnson's 1964 Gulf of Tonkin response and Carter's 1980 Iranian hostage rescue mission), no ethnic appeals antagonizing our allies (as Wilson in 1916 antagonized the British in order to please the American Irish), no crude political machinations (like Nixon in 1972 at Watergate), no abandonment of programs that lack vocal constituencies—like increasing foreign aid and trade, reducing deficits and inflation, closing surplus federal installations and, above all, raising taxes—no need to dazzle the voters with time-consuming world travel or military tours or emotional speeches, and no dilution or prostitution of policy in order to raise campaign money, woo public opinion or avoid controversy.

"Nothing is more dangerous," Winston Churchill once wrote regarding the responsibility of a political leader, "than to live in the temperamental atmosphere of a Gallup Poll, always taking one's . . . political temperature. . . . There is only one duty, only one safe course, and that is to try to be right."

Still another advantage of not seeking reelection, as well as not exercising party control, will be the absence of any need for the new President to bring into the White House with him campaign aides, advance men and representatives of various interest groups who are inexperienced in Congressional, national and international affairs. This will present him with a marvelous opportunity to both raise the quality and reduce the quantity of the White House staff.

Those selected by the President and Vice-President for that Coalition White House staff, including in particular the Chief of Staff (if any), the National Security Adviser, the top Domestic Policy Adviser, the Counsel and the Chief of Congressional Liaison, should be equally divided between the two major political parties and serve jointly both the President and Vice-President. Like the members of the Coalition Cabinet, they should be experienced and moderate.

Presidents Carter and Reagan included among their White House assistants individuals with little knowledge of the way Washington works (and doesn't work). They were not the first. Somehow a nation whose citizens would not dream of hiring an inexperienced heart surgeon or an unlicensed tree surgeon permits its President to rely on amateurs for advice about vital national and international issues. Foreign governments, in the midst of negotiations or other relationships with us, and more accustomed to the tradition of "shadow cabinets" which are instantly ready to make decisions upon assuming power, understandably object to the delays and uncertainties they encounter while each new group of euphoric and inexperienced White House aides educates itself on the issues and settles its own feuds. In the Coalition White House, men and women from both parties with maturity and judgment could be a force for unity in the administration, instead of a source of dissension and contention. As former Presidential aide George Reedy has written: "It is possible for a President to assemble a staff of mature men [*sic*] who are past the period of inordinate ambition . . . but this rarely, if ever, happens."

A much smaller White House staff is less likely to antagonize the Coalition Cabinet by duplicating departmental roles, making or misstating policy, undertaking or undermining diplomatic missions, or administering operations. Friction between the Secretary of State and the President's National Security Adviser, which for fifteen years or more has recurringly given this country a split-screen image around the world, is not inevitable if the President will make clear that the Secretary is the government's chief diplomatic spokesman and that the Adviser is to confine his advice to the President.

A much smaller White House staff (consistent with a deficit-reducing administration) is also less likely to increase the President's isolation, to abuse power, to exercise unsupervised authority, to fragment policy-making, to disclose internal dissension, to complain to the press, and to fuss over who has the President's ear, his confidence or the adjoining office.

As a further demonstration of both unity and continuity, the Coalition President should establish by Executive Order a Council of Elders composed of our retired Presidents, Secretaries of State, Speakers of the House and Senate Majority Leaders—roughly a dozen experienced individuals from both parties, to be convened regularly by the President and Vice-President in person, for both briefings and consultations. No votes would be taken, no decisions would be delegated, no joint statements would be expected. But this largely untapped pool of wisdom could be an invaluable source of advice.

Drawing upon the experience of those who have been there before, and working with a knowledgeable staff and Cabinet, will also help the Coalition President save time. Time will be his enemy. Under normal circumstances, a traditional one-party President, if limited to one term, would be hard-pressed to complete his work in four years. New Executive and Legislative measures must be prepared, proposed, considered, enacted, funded and implemented. Each of those steps can take a year. Nevertheless, the first-term accomplishments of Wilson and FDR, among others, show what can be done in that time period. A new Coalition President, who knows from the start that he must do it all in four years, should be able to translate his unique bipartisan support into a fruitful term. Certainly he will have far more capacity at his command than Wilson or FDR ever had to communicate quickly with his aides, allies and adversaries and to analyze instantly complex economic, scientific and military data.

Above all, he will have four full years focused on creative and productive work, without losing time at the start as the result of an inexperienced White House staff and Cabinet, and without diverting time at the end to his reelection campaign. Because he has renounced his right to another four years in office, his every act and statement during the second half of his term will not be viewed as critically by the opposition or as cynically by the Congress. There will be no need for key decisions in both branches of government to be shaped, as they have these past two years, more by political calendars and considerations than by national needs. By avoiding, in the second half of his term especially, the loss of Congressional confidence and support inherent in a reelection campaign, the Coalition President will be better able to devote his own time, energy and staff to policy questions instead of polls, and to attending Cabinet meetings instead of fund-raisers.

In short, we will have a President willing to stay in the political kitchen and take the heat—to "try to be right," as Churchill advised, to tackle tough problems on which he cannot "win" politically, to block federal outlays cherished by the special-interest PACs, and to set forth national goals and values that transcend personal political concerns.

If he can do that, he may well have the satisfaction of becoming the first ex-President since Theodore Roosevelt to retain a significant leadership role in public and political affairs. (Because he is able to limit his public appearances as President, he also increases his chances of living to be an ex-President.) Whatever criticism he endures for taking that "heat," he can be consoled by the knowledge that history usually ranks highest those Presidents who were willing to bear the brunt of politically controversial actions.

If his Coalition Government can lead this country into a new era of less dangerous U.S.–Soviet relations, less burdensome federal deficits, and more prosperous economic competitiveness, no doubt successor administrations and generations will have an easier time in that "Promised Land" than he will have in his four years. But, like Moses, the Coalition President would be honored for showing the rest of us the way.

# 6

# BOTH ADVICE AND CONSENT

*In 1910, David Lloyd George, then a young member of the British Cabinet deeply concerned about his country's problems, recommended that they be settled "by the active co-operation of both the Great Parties in the State." In a lengthy private memorandum that he presented to Prime Minister Asquith and a few others, he urged temporary adoption of a step that had long been viewed in London with skepticism if not disdain—coalition. "This country," Lloyd George wrote, "has gained a good deal from the conflict and rivalry of Parties, and it will gain a good deal more in the future from the same cause; but I cannot help thinking that the time has arrived for a truce."*

*He then listed those issues before the country and Parliament that he felt "illustrated the difficulty of dealing with some of these problems except by joint action"—for example, compulsory military training ("no Party dare touch it, because of the violent prejudices which would be excited"). Continued legislative neglect of these problems, he said, "may end in national impoverishment, if not insolvency." Yet:*

*at the present moment the questions which are of the most
vital importance to the well-being of the great community
are all questions which are not only capable of being settled
by the joint action of the two great Parties without involving
any sacrifice of principle on the part of either, but which can
better be settled by such cooperation than by the normal
working of Party machinery.*

*Lloyd George regarded the traditional party battles in
Parliament, given the context of the times, as irrelevant
and unnecessarily distracting. That was precisely how the
traditional party leaders in Parliament regarded his proposal. It died.*

*In time, the exigencies of war led the United Kingdom
into the rudimentary coalition of 1915 and then in 1916
into David Lloyd George's own Coalition of National Unity for the remainder of the war and postwar emergency.
Whatever its later faults, that coalition's wartime unifica-
tion of political command—an approach emulated even
more successfully by Winston Churchill's coalition government during the Second World War—bore out the predic-
tion contained in Lloyd George's 1910 memorandum:
"Such a Government, representing as it would not a fragment, but the whole nation, would undoubtedly enhance
the prestige of this country abroad."*

COALITION Government in the United States will not
and should not diminish either the positive or the negative powers of Congress in its relations with the President. Nor can Coalition Government in this country
succeed unless Congress is a full-fledged participant.

No new law, Constitutional amendment or other

action by Congress is required to put the plan set forth in this book into effect. On the contrary, should a deadlocked Congress be unable or for some reason unwilling to work with the Executive Branch in promulgating a bipartisan program, the Coalition President and Cabinet would not be without capacity to act on their own, particularly in the conduct of foreign affairs, the reduction of federal spending, the appointment of advisory councils, and the motivation of American management, workers and consumers. But if the Congress responds to coalition in the Executive by improving its own efforts at compromise and cooperation, if it is ready to assert an active role in this new effort, then the exercise of its power over funding, appointments, legislation and international agreements will be critical to the Coalition President's success.

The key is to develop a properly balanced relationship. Better the inevitable inconveniences of Legislative-Executive collaboration than the perils of either submission or confrontation. A weak Fillmore or Buchanan meekly deferring to the Congress, even in domestic affairs, is as inconsistent with our Constitutional design as a Lyndon Johnson or Richard Nixon seeking to avoid and disregard the Congress, especially in foreign affairs.

Even under the Coalition approach, collaboration between the Legislative and Executive branches will not be easy. The views of 535 legislators from two parties, two houses and fifty states are inevitably more independent and fragmented, and less easily compromised and coordinated, than those of a dozen Cabinet members. As one veteran Congressman summed up his attitude toward bipartisanship some years ago: "Sometimes I coalesce and sometimes I don't."

To succeed with the Congress, a Coalition President will need to do more than voice the usual self-serving appeals for bipartisan support of his policies. The very concept of Coalition requires his adoption of the following measures:

## 1. *Briefings and Consultations*

An uninformed Congress is more likely to be an unhappy and uncooperative Congress. An informed and involved Congress will be less likely to block or overturn Administration initiatives. As Republican Senator Arthur Vandenberg (actually quoting Harold Stassen) liked to say in the postwar era of foreign policy bipartisanship under Democrat Harry Truman: "We want to be copilots in the takeoffs as well as the crash landings." This means getting Congress involved early, deeply, quietly and regularly in the design of policy as well as its legislative wording and strategy.

Briefings cannot be sporadic, belated, partial or partisan. Congressmen outside the President's political party should never for that reason be left outside the President's briefing room. The President's weekly breakfast with the legislative leaders of both houses should always include those of both parties, not merely his own.

A useful precedent to reestablish was Secretary of State Cyrus Vance's effort during the Iran and Afghanistan crises to brief the Congressional leadership every day and all interested members once a week. (This practice was remembered by Republican Congressional leaders in 1983 when the Reagan Administration failed to inform even the President's own party in Congress about its Central America military maneuvers until well after the press had the story.)

In short, both branches will need to make an extra effort to go that extra mile along Pennsylvania Avenue. Woodrow Wilson did so literally—not only as the first President since John Adams to deliver his State of the Union Message in person, but also as the first President since Lincoln to use with any frequency the stately President's Room across from the Senate Chamber to meet and persuade key legislators and review proposed legislation with them. That could be done again.

## 2. *Legislation*

Congress lost last year one of its most familiar tools for placing limits on Executive Branch conduct: the "legislative veto." The United States Supreme Court declared it unconstitutional. Immediately, predictions of excessively restrictive substitutes or unfettered Executive discretion were heard in the land. Four years of unusual Coalition cooperation on legislation and of abnormal trust between the two branches, while new legislative safeguards against Executive blank checks are evolved, would be in everyone's interest.

Many members of Congress, particularly those concerned that the more provincial pressures in their constituencies could cause their defeat, are usually less willing and able than the President to take a long, statesmanlike view on emotion-laden national issues. A bipartisan Cabinet, and particularly a President not seeking reelection, should be far more willing to stand this political heat and accept the burdens and blame of national controversy. By deft political footwork and public messages, the Coalition President, in consultation with Congressional leaders and his Cabinet, should be able to propose and draft new legislation on politically sensitive issues in a manner that majorities in both houses can support with the full assurance that he, not they, will bear the brunt of any attack.

One method particularly suited to use by a bipartisan Coalition Cabinet working closely with Congressional leaders is the legislative "package," the device used in 1983 to preserve the Social Security Trust Fund. Under this approach, a series of compromises, each of them essential to some Congressional or constituent group but unappetizing to another, can be combined in a carefully balanced bill accompanied by a credible warning that the entire bill must be passed intact lest the deletion or expansion of any one item alter that balance and cause its defeat. Faced simply with a choice of voting up or down a measure that members know must not fail, the Congress grits its collective teeth and reluctantly acquiesces, castigating the Executive for forcing this choice but happy to be able to make clear to all constituents and contributors that the blame lies elsewhere. A Coalition President, not running for reelection, will be happy to take the blame and to use this means of playing off against each other Washington's usually influential special-interest and single-issue organizations. Because this device restricts the normal legislative process of debate and amendment, frequent use of the package approach may be resisted by legislative leaders except during this extraordinary and limited Coalition period.

### 3. *Presidential Appointments*

The Constitution calls for the advice as well as the consent of the Senate on Presidential nominations. A Coalition President should adhere literally to that standard by reviewing with the Senate leadership, including appropriate committee seniors from both parties, his "short list" of potential nominees for Cabinet, sub-Cabinet and other major agency posts. (This practice will be particularly appropriate for the Supreme Court, where the next President will almost surely have the opportunity to make lifetime appointments filling a majority of the Court's nine seats—an unusual power over the next generation that should be exercised in a bipartisan manner.)

The Congress, which by this process should have more confidence in this set of appointees than in any other, can also reduce rancor—and make high government service more attractive—by minimizing the abusive hearings and excessive public disclosures that cause some prospective nominees, particularly in the business and professional communities, to decline the honor. Some prospects willing to divest themselves of all assets presenting a potential conflict, and willing to accept a sharp drop in income, are less willing to be embarrassed in public by how much money they have earned or saved (or, in some cases, how little).

The bipartisan Coalition period will also be an appropriate time for the Executive and Legislative branches to make permanent arrangements for placing particular agencies that need no partisan rule under long-term nonpartisan career officials, as has already been done with the Federal Reserve Board and the Federal Bureau of Investigation. Among those agencies that should join this nonpartisan list are the Central Intelligence Agency, the Environmental Protection Administration, the Veterans Administration, and even the Department of Education. A bipartisan period of government would also be the time to clear up the anomalous situation of the Civil Rights Commission by giving its bipartisan members fixed, long-term but not permanent Presidential appointments.

## 4. *Treaties*

The Constitution also calls for the advice as well as the consent of the Senate with regard to treaties. Here, too, the Coalition President must invite the early and active participation of Senate leaders from both parties, if the Coalition is to make solid progress on arms control and other key international issues.

In theory, it can be argued that foreign policy is too sensitive to be subjected to domestic political pressure from Congress. In practice, some Presidents prior to Watergate sought an executive monopoly on foreign policy decision-making, utilizing covert operations, the overclassification of documents, and secret decisions and missions to exclude Congressional participation and oversight. But both that theory and that practice also exclude the press, the nongovernmental experts, the concerned citizens and the consent of the governed. That is not the way to produce public confidence, a government consensus or foreign policy continuity.

Instead, whether the policy under the proposed new Coalition Government is called bipartisan, nonpartisan (Cordell Hull's preference) or unpartisan (Arthur Vandenberg's invention), bringing Congress explicitly into the formulation, evaluation and implementation as well as the ratification of a Coalition foreign policy could produce the most harmony and progress in this area since our first Secretary of State, Thomas Jefferson, with a total departmental staff of eight, personally handled all Congressional contacts.

Today the wounds of Vietnam are not fully healed and are in danger of being reopened by Central America. Partisan maneuvering to gain advantage or escape blame in world affairs is still common. Nevertheless, the time for a new foreign policy consensus may be at hand. As Flora Lewis has written: "A bipartisan policy would separate the mainstream from the noisy fringes." Within that mainstream of both parties, liberal guilt and conservative paranoia remaining from Vietnam have diminished, dovish naiveté about Soviet power and goodwill has diminished, and hawkish overconfidence about the infallibility of American military solutions has diminished. Consensus now may be possible.

The Coalition President, following the precedent of his earliest predecessors from George Washington to Andrew Jackson, must be willing to consult the Senate in advance on all major international negotiations. He must be willing to accept suggestions for change from, and to share any acclaim with, the Congress and both parties. Most important, he must include key Senators from both parties—and Congressmen as well—on this country's negotiating team at the arms control talks and on delegations to other international conferences.

Because the Constitution forbids any member of Congress from accepting an Executive Branch appointment while remaining a member of the Legislative Branch, and because Congressmen will resist any appearance that they have been either co-opted or offered only token gestures, a middle-ground role somewhere between observer and Executive Branch official must be found without destroying the prospects for a coherent U.S. delegation presentation. Congressmen can be delegation advisers; or they can be appointed to the delegation by Congress to represent Congress; or they can be informal members of the delegation—all of these have been tried in the last half century. (In the early days of the Republic, those members of Congress given diplomatic responsibilities resigned from Congress; but that is not now deemed necessary.)

Carter in 1978 asked Congress to name advisers to the SALT II negotiations. Kennedy in 1963 included members of the Senate Foreign Relations Committee in the Moscow mission for the Limited Nuclear Test Ban Treaty. Truman in the postwar years, following Roosevelt's 1944 precedents, set the best example for giving legislators from both parties a share in the actual responsibility for conducting international negotiations. He appointed Senators Tom Connally and Arthur Vandenberg as delegates to the first General As-

sembly of the United Nations and as delegates to the
Council of Foreign Ministers writing peace treaties for
the Balkan States and Italy. He named Senator Warren
Austin and others as delegates to the Inter-American
Conference in Rio de Janeiro that led to the formation
of the Organization of American States.

Arthur Schlesinger, Jr., has written that inclusion of
Republican Congressmen in the NATO, Greek-Turkey
Aid, Marshall Plan and other negotiations was accom-
plished only by exaggerating the Soviet menace and
discouraging Congressional debate. Yet he recognized
the success of this approach and Truman's reasons for
utilizing it, reasons not inapposite today. "The bipartisan foreign policy was not a good idea," wrote Schlesinger. "It was only a necessity."

# 7

# AN ECONOMIC CONSENSUS

*In 1933, President Franklin D. Roosevelt, having led the Democratic party to its first victory in sixteen years, was not enthusiastic about bringing in non-Democrats to run the federal government, despite his bipartisan rhetoric. On the contrary, nine out of his ten Cabinet appointments were members of the FRBC Club—"for Roosevelt before Chicago"—an all-time high in the coincidence of preconvention support with Cabinet qualification. Nevertheless, he recognized that some innovation in governmental affairs was required to avoid the total collapse of our economy and institutions in the Great Depression. He further recognized that the traditional hostilities between a Democratic administration and business, and between business and labor, and between labor and farmers, and between farmers and consumers, were virtually irrelevant under those emergency conditions.*

*He thus improvised a National Recovery Administration and an Agricultural Adjustment Administration, which brought these private interests into the actual regulation of the economy. "Each group," he said, "must think of itself as a part of a greater whole, one piece in a large design." At the same time, he eschewed partisan political activities, even going so far as to refuse to attend the various state Democratic Day Dinners in 1934.*

*The original NRA and AAA were experiments too fragile and hastily slapped together to last, much less to fulfill all their objectives. They fell before legal, practical and political assaults, and FDR himself resumed his party role. But his extraordinary early efforts to enlist the private sector in these pilot programs did help to restore hope in this country, to get wheels turning, and to lay the groundwork for subsequent government programs.*

THE President elected in 1984 will not face an American economy in a state of depression. He will find it in a crucial state of transition. The four years following his Inauguration will determine whether we can master our Budget deficits or they enslave our economy, whether we can rise to the challenge of international competition or sink into further stagnation and instability, whether our banking system can prevent the collapse of major Third World governments or will collapse along with them, whether we can keep open and expand the channels of world trade or fall prey to the pressures of protectionism and economic warfare. Action or inaction by the federal government during these next several years will not alone determine whether the transition leads to growth or decline. But it will make a substantial difference.

If Coalition is adopted, more cooperation between the two political parties and between the Executive and Legislative branches of government, and less turmoil and turnover in the Cabinet agencies responsible for economic matters, will help provide the continuity and certainty in economic policy we need during this period. But if it is to be a period of rethinking, retooling and readjustment to the new national and international economic scene, then the recommendations, harmonization and collaboration of the private sector must be obtained as well. Government cannot and should not do it all.

The Coalition President should therefore establish by Executive Order a new National Council of Economic Cooperation and Coordination. Its private-sector members would be drawn not only from industry and labor but also from finance, agriculture, education, consumer and public-interest organizations, including those representing the poor. Its public-sector members would be drawn from the Coalition Cabinet, the federal Office of Management and Budget, the Federal Reserve Board, the President's Council of Economic Advisers, the Congress, and state and local governments. The President would personally conduct each session. (It is not necessary that he have formal training in economics. Herbert Hoover did.) Outside specialists could be invited to make presentations; but membership of the Council, if its meetings are to be productive, should be kept to a maximum of twenty men and women around the Council table.

Those chosen by the President from the private sector, with the advice of their respective constituencies and with the greatest care, must be men and women able to represent the long-range interests of those constituents and not merely their slogans, able to devote enormous blocks of time to Council meetings and not send assistants, able to disagree with the President and each other whenever necessary, able to understand the needs of other interests and sectors and the nation as a whole, and able ultimately to compromise on a consensus compendium of policies and practices that best serve those national needs, a new "social compact" for America.

Tripartite business-labor-public panels to advise the President on economic matters are not new. President Carter proposed one in 1980. One of President Reagan's little-noticed commissions, in the mass of 1983 commissions, was a group asked to study industrial competitiveness. Another was asked how to revive the steel industry. But the Council contemplated here would be far more than another blue-ribbon advisory commission. The Coalition President would be seeking more than the usual one-shot report. He would be seeking the participation of Council members on behalf of their constituent groups in not only the formulation but also the implementation of national economic policy and in the creation of a national consensus behind that policy.

Changes in law and regulation would still require the Constitutionally mandated action of Congress and the President. But Council members, in addition to their role in developing these changes, would be responsible for seeking private cooperation with those laws and regulations, and, of greater importance, voluntary adoption of price, wage, profit, marketing, research, product and other decisions forming a part of the social compact.

A similar collaborative effort convened by the Governor of New York a few years ago saved New York City from fiscal ruin. Many foreign governments—notably in Japan and several West European countries—have successfully involved business and labor as collaborators in public decision-making instead of adversaries in the private arena.

Given this country's very different size, diversity, history and "competitive ethic," as George Shultz terms it, a Japanese-type culture of cooperation will be difficult for us to develop. In the past, American labor and management have given little more than lip service to efforts of this kind. But this time, for the first time, they will be approached by a bipartisan Coalition President. They will know that such an Administration is not seeking to exploit them for partisan purposes. They will know that all other groups in the economy are being asked to make comparable concessions, and that this period of compromise and collaboration will last no more than four years. They will be concerned about the state of the economy and they will be concerned about antagonizing a strong President and Cabinet backed by both parties and working closely with the Congress. I believe the Coalition President will be able to obtain meaningful and accommodative participation from all groups.

Similar participation must be obtained from the Federal Reserve Board. Its cherished independence would not prevent it from coordinating its policies and actions with those of the Administration and new Council. Conversely, a four-year period of clear and consistent signals on the economy from the Administration, unknown in the last two decades, and similar clarity on the President's choice for Federal Reserve Chairman, will better enable the "Fed" to fine-tune its tools of monetary and credit restraint.

The most urgent and difficult task facing the new Council will be reduction of the federal budget deficit—raising tax revenues and cutting expenditures in the context of national and international economic trends. The pressures on the Council will all be in the opposite direction. But for every new tax incentive offered as part of our battle to be competitive internationally—to encourage savings over excessive consumption, for example, or to encourage investment in new productive assets instead of paper acquisitions, or to encourage research and retraining, or to encourage more educational contributions for those purposes, all of which are undoubtedly desirable—each group represented around that Council table will need to find existing, equally costly (and no doubt equally cherished) tax incentives, exemptions and preferences that it would be willing to forgo, merely to keep the deficit from growing larger.

Similarly, for every new spending program offered in the interests of a stronger economy—to provide loans for ailing industries, new technologies or plant modernization; to increase grants for education in mathematics, science or computer studies; to expand funding for research, development and retraining; to establish a new "economic NASA" to focus federal capital assistance on rehabilitating and retooling old industries or developing and promoting new ones; to increase export subsidies and marketing activities, all of which are undoubtedly desirable—each group represented around that table must find existing, equally costly (and no doubt equally cherished) Budget items that it would be willing to forgo, merely to keep the deficit from growing larger.

But keeping the deficit from growing larger will not be enough. A freeze in federal spending will not be enough. Deep reductions in that deficit will be urgently required, and no one's sacred cow or traditional pork barrel will be safe. No doubt, one side of the table will call for reducing the deficit by cutting defense spending and closing tax loopholes; and the other side will call for cutting welfare grants, food stamps and bureaucratic waste. Both sides will then call for the Federal Reserve Board to adopt policies accommodating a higher deficit. But once those speeches are over, and all Council members accept the fact that all those cuts combined will never be sufficient and that the Federal Reserve Board will never be that passive, they will face the painful task of strengthening the tax base and reducing the federal tax deduction and spending programs benefiting every group represented around that table.

No doubt, cries of "centralized planning" will greet any Council attempts at coordination. No new bureaucracy, no monolithic national planning agency, no unaccountable power is contemplated or necessary for this Council. No government force can tell an American businessman where to invest, or an American consumer how much to save, or an American worker how hard to work. No purpose is served in trying to substitute government for the marketplace on those decisions where the latter's judgment should be determinative.

But every Administration, whether liberal or conservative, makes important budget, tax, capital allocation and legislative decisions based on long-range forecasts of the economy and its own fiscal targets. Every Administration makes decisions on tariffs and trade, agricultural subsidies, tax incentives, antitrust philosophy and government procurement with an eye on the strengths and weaknesses of particular sectors of the economy. Customarily these decisions are made without sufficient information, consistency or analysis, and without an examination of long-term national trends and priorities.

The new Council need not result in more government intervention. It should produce better coordination of both information and action by both government and private decision-makers. It should produce more cooperation between the two. If those around the Council table can harmonize for four years their customarily clashing interests—at least temporarily relating profit, price and payroll demands to productivity, subordinating tax and spending requests to deficit reduction, matching unused industrial capacity with unused capital and human resources, and unused educational resources with unfulfilled job retraining needs, balancing fiscal and monetary policies with national long-term economic strategy, reallocating existing tax preferences and government loans to fit the rapid changes in our economy—that kind of consensus and coherence would dramatically improve confidence in both our government and our economy.

This is not the place to prescribe the Council's final decisions. It may wish to formulate a new "national industrial policy," providing more direct government incentives to those technologically advanced industries most likely to maintain U.S. competitive strength. It may formulate a new "incomes policy," using either carrots or sticks to keep wage and price movements noninflationary. It may wish to call for a new federal agency like the old Reconstruction Finance Corporation, providing loans and other temporary assistance to distressed industries capable of recouping their competitive position. It may wish to recommend shifting all or part of the federal Budget to a multiyear cycle, enhancing economic certainty and continuity. It may wish to recommend drastic changes in federal regulations, antitrust laws, export controls, education finance and job security. Or, after extensive study, it may wish to recommend none of these initiatives.

One measure certain to be under consideration, once private interests are invited to the government decision-making table, is the imposition of restrictions on certain foreign imports, presumably in exchange for adjustments by labor and management in those industries. Protectionism, by inviting retaliation, shielding inefficiency and penalizing consumers, can only make more difficult the long-term economic growth without inflation that our industry and labor most need. But a one-term Coalition President actually in the process of obtaining a restructuring of American industry through the voluntary cooperation of management and labor may try to convince our trading partners and our consumers that a temporary breathing spell is needed during this transition to more balanced competition and that it will in fact be only temporary. Nevertheless, promulgation by the new Council of import quotas in selected industries, clearly expiring no later than the end of the Coalition's four-year term and dependent on industry and labor's accepting other essential changes, could be justified only if required to avert more far-reaching and permanent protectionism.

In this same vein, other temporary agreements—with as many of our key industrial and trading allies as may be willing—should be pursued by the Coalition and the Council to make the transition period one of international economic stability: agreements fixing parameters for participating nations for the movement of interest rates, exchange rates and monetary growth rates; coordinating their energy prices, practices and alternative source policies; equalizing their tax, credit and other export subsidies; reconciling their export controls; and generally meshing more clearly their respective battles against inflation, unemployment, budget deficits, balance of payments deficits and other economic ills. The urgent need for collaboration on Third World debt and credit problems has already been stressed. Beginning this unprecedented effort of international economic collaboration and harmonization with a small group of allies may be more practical than attempting a grand concord with all industrialized nations at the start.

So far-reaching a series of temporary international agreements will require formulation of a coherent foreign economic policy for this country by the Coalition Cabinet and new National Council. We have not had one for many years. It may require as well some restriction on each country's freedom of action. But many governments borrowing from the International Monetary Fund, including Britain and Italy as well as scores of developing nations, have as a condition for those loans accepted temporary restrictions, some of them vastly unpopular, on their economic conduct. The United States and other industrialized nations, if they recognize the potential economic disaster inherent in merely perpetuating the status quo, should similarly be able to accept some self-discipline for the common good.

An economic consensus among even a few allies is a lot to ask. So is an economic consensus here at home. Drastic changes, on a scale comparable to those instituted by Roosevelt fifty years ago, may be required. But despite all the attacks on FDR from the Far Right, more than one historian has recognized in retrospect that Roosevelt's innovative efforts "saved the capitalist system in the United States."

Our economic system today, in dire peril of being crushed by deficits at home and competition abroad, is once again in need of an innovative rescue. Coalition Government with private-sector participation is one answer.

# 8

# FREEZE AND THAW

*In the early 1940s, as America was drawn into the Second World War, President Franklin D. Roosevelt adopted on international issues the nonpartisan approach he employed during his first two years of office on domestic economic issues. "These perilous days," he said, "demand cooperation between us without a trace of partisanship."*

*Nearly all Presidents say that, as previously noted, because they interpret bipartisanship to mean support for the President from the opposition party. Roosevelt, the founder of the modern Democratic party and a spirited campaigner, was not by nature either nonpartisan or bipartisan. Particularly after Republican resistance to his reciprocal trade and selective service legislation, he was no exception to the parade of twentieth-century Presidents who preferred to conduct the nation's foreign affairs without involving the Congress, much less the other party. His Secretary of State, Cordell Hull, was a crusty Democrat who had little love for Republicans and even less desire to let them share the credit for any Administration successes.*

*But war meant sacrifice, and FDR and Hull recognized the need to sacrifice their preference for a solely partisan and Presidential foreign policy. Roosevelt appointed Henry Stimson, a Republican veteran of the Taft and Hoover Cabinets, to be Secretary of War. He named Frank Knox, the Republican Vice-Presidential nominee in 1936, to be Secretary of the Navy. Republican Senators like Arthur Vandenberg and Warren Austin, Republican Congressmen like Charles Eaton, Republican Governors like Harold Stassen, Republican foreign policy experts like John Foster Dulles, were not only consulted but also appointed to United States delegations to the international conferences then preparing for the postwar peace process.*

*The 1940 Republican Presidential nominee, Wendell Willkie, willingly accepted a role as a roving ambassador abroad and (much as Stephen Douglas rallied his Democratic followers to support Lincoln's war policies) served also as a unifying speaker at home. The State Department worked closely with the Foreign Affairs Committee in each house to produce bipartisan agreements on foreign relief and rehabilitation assistance. In the 1944 Presidential contest, both Roosevelt and his Republican opponent, Thomas E. Dewey, agreed not to make campaign speeches focusing on United States policy abroad. Roosevelt, convinced that this bipartisan approach strengthened his bargaining power, took fifty copies of a Vandenberg speech to the Great Power Conference at Yalta in 1945.*

*This spirit of bipartisanship in foreign affairs was not adopted by every political leader of the time; it broke down on occasions even during the war; and it vanished quickly when the postwar period ended. But it helped provide a remarkable degree of unity on those issues on which unity was urgently required. It was a time, to use Roosevelt's earlier words, for "thinking about government and not merely about party. . . . [I]f we have the right kind of people, the party label does not mean so very much."*

A MORE unified White House, Executive Branch, federal government and nation are clearly within the reach of a one-term Coalition President. Greater economic and political unity within the Western Alliance can also be achieved with some major effort by both the U.S. Coalition and other members. But East-West harmony, or, more specifically, better U.S.–Soviet relations, will not be easily attained even by a Coalition.

Decades of discord and distrust cannot be permanently reversed in only four years. Consensus proposals from a United States Government finally speaking with one voice will still have to contend with the realities of Soviet power and expansionism and historical Soviet security concerns about its neighbors. Nothing this country says or does, as indicated by our experience with the "détente" illusions of a decade ago, will cause Moscow to embrace human rights, adopt a pluralistic society, accept hostile or even unreliable governments in Eastern Europe or Afghanistan, or refrain from seeking to win friends, influence governments and support Marxist revolutions throughout the Third World. As Andrei Sakharov has written about Western hopes for peace-loving and progressive thoughts in the Soviet camp: "Objective reality is much more complicated. . . . [A] passionate aspiration for peace . . . does not exclude the possibility of a tragic outcome."

Engaging in the self-criticism that is a hallmark of a democratic society, we sometimes forget that the United States is not the only superpower whose leadership has engaged in harsh rhetoric about the other, is subject to domestic political pressures for more arms instead of arms control, and sees fundamental conflicts in the interests and perceptions of the U.S. and the U.S.S.R. that make even limited agreement difficult. Nor would any strategic arms reduction agreement within the furthest range of twentieth-century probability eliminate either side's ability to destroy the other. International arms control, like domestic gun control, is highly desirable, but not a complete answer. (Missiles don't kill people; people kill people.)

Nevertheless, reducing for four years the element of partisan politics in U.S. foreign policy, and establishing at the helm a Coalition President and National Security Council with no reelection concerns, could make a difference. It should at least make it more possible for this country to seek a more constructive U.S.– Soviet relationship based upon mutual restraint and reciprocity instead of constant confrontation.

Such a relationship, if consistently maintained and strengthened, could over time benefit the U.S. Budget, our industrial investment and our relations with the Western Alliance. It is not likely to diminish the mutual differences between the two superpowers, and probably not our mutual distrust, much less the ideological, political and economic competition between our two systems, particularly among Third World nations. But the United States and the West, because they are better able than Moscow to offer those Third World nations what they need most—access to world markets, economic development assistance, and a meaningful pledge of noninterference in their political independence and diversity—have no reason to fear that ideological, political and economic competition.

History's first important step toward strategic arms control—the Limited Nuclear Test Ban Treaty of 1963—was facilitated by a unilateral initiative by the United States: namely, a Presidential declaration of a moratorium on all further nuclear testing in the atmosphere, so long as the Soviet Union did likewise. This was a calculated risk, a gamble that our unilateral initiative would sufficiently increase the prospects for a formal binding treaty to offset any domestic criticism of unilateralism. The gamble paid off. The treaty was signed.

President Anwar Sadat of Egypt made the same kind of gamble, measuring the degree of risk against the prospect of results, in initiating his dramatic peace mission to Jerusalem. A one-term Coalition President, if he can obtain bipartisan backing from his Vice-President, Cabinet and Congressional leaders, could undertake similar initiatives with less risk of domestic displeasure and no worries about being termed "soft" in a reelection campaign.

A moratorium of the kind initiated in 1963—a promise to refrain from certain activity so long as the other side does likewise—is, when and if adopted by the other side, in effect an informal "freeze." Proposals for a nuclear weapons freeze have been hotly debated over the past few years in this country and Western Europe. The arguments against such a freeze have not all come from those who like to cast aspersions on the loyalty or intelligence of freeze proponents and indeed to cast doubt on any serious arms control agreement of any kind. Because it would perpetuate existing dangerous and excessive nuclear weapons stockpiles, because it could not prevent destabilizing technological breakthroughs or breakdowns over a period of time, and because it could not assure permanent strategic equivalence between the superpowers, a freeze—although far superior to the present unabated arms race—makes most sense if it is of limited duration, if like the 1963 testing moratorium it is at most a first step that will be withdrawn if it does not lead to genuine arms reductions.

A Coalition President, with the backing of his bipartisan Cabinet, after consultation with Congressional leaders, and after quiet and informal talks between the two superpowers, could declare that this country, for the remainder of his single four-year term and no longer, would after a specified date halt the production, testing and deployment of strategic nuclear weapons (including the MX missile and the B-1 bomber), the production of plutonium, and the testing of anti-satellite and other space weapons, and comply with the provisions (other than the 1985 expiration date) of the unratified SALT II Treaty, provided that the Soviet Union does likewise, and provided that negotiations proceed promptly on a series of treaties to assure and expand these informal commitments. He could further declare that, unless those binding comprehensive treaties are concluded by the end of the Coalition President's term, each such freeze would expire.

The concept of limiting the duration of a particular arms control agreement or provision, in anticipation of a more far-reaching successor agreement, is not new, having been included in both SALT I and SALT II. The very brevity of such an agreement's duration reduces any incentive to terminate or cheat. The likelihood of any violations of these potential "freezes" being detected, and the desire to keep the other side bound by the freeze, to woo public favor in Western Europe, Japan and Third World countries, and presumably to obtain a comprehensive agreement at the end of the process, would also discourage cheating, once such a moratorium was accepted by both parties.

But would the Soviet Union accept? Much depends on developments between the time of this writing and the time of such a declaration, on Soviet perceptions of the Coalition President, on Soviet confidence in its own means of verification, and on internal Soviet pressures favoring and opposing such agreements. Its leaders have asserted support for a bilateral nuclear weapons freeze. A freeze on the total number of land-based ICBM launchers was included in the SALT I agreement.

More important, there is reason to believe (at this writing) that the next several years will be a time of transition for the Soviet Union as well as the United States; that its current leadership is cautious, and preoccupied with domestic economic and political adjustments as well as with problems on their borders; and that a more rational U.S.–U.S.S.R. relationship may be regarded by the Kremlin as preferable to the present relationship, with its heavy costs and high risks.

A unilaterally initiated but reciprocally observed nuclear freeze might thus provide a "cooling-off period" that would open the way to a series of genuine long-term arms control agreements providing comprehensive bans and reductions of a long list of nuclear weapons systems. The negotiation of such agreements, assuring equality, verifiability and stability as well as a reduction in numbers, will require far more time than the ten days spent in Moscow in 1963 negotiating the Limited Test Ban Treaty. The bargaining will not be easy once the parties reach, as they must, those particular areas of nuclear strength in which each side has traditionally considered itself "ahead" of the other. Nevertheless, if both sides can negotiate with an intensity not shown in recent years, if they can set aside all the rhetoric about essentially meaningless number comparisons, if they can downgrade the role of their respective arms control "theologians," who speak in terms no policy-maker can understand, then these comprehensive agreements can be completed and ratified before the Coalition's mandate expires on January 20, 1989.

It has not been unusual for Soviet leaders, when American Presidential elections approach, to drag their feet in negotiations, in hopes of getting a better deal from the next President, or (like the Iranians in 1980) of avoiding boosting the reelection chances of a President or party they do not like. But the Coalition President will not be seeking reelection. His administration will not represent a single party. More important, he will be uniquely positioned to turn the "wait until after the election" game the other way. With bipartisan backing and no reelection concerns, he will be offering the Soviets a greater certainty of agreement than they could expect to get from his successor. If they delay needlessly, any agreement will face the usual U.S. clash of partisan views and ambitions in 1989—after the nuclear freeze has ended in disappointment. If the Soviets want an agreement, they won't drag their feet.

In the meantime, a similar approach could be made on other areas of present tension and potential collaboration. A permanent (until January 20, 1989) U.S.–U.S.S.R. Commission on Reduction of Tensions, with a bipartisan U.S. delegation on which Congress is represented, could through a series of subcommittees explore a host of issues on a "joint and several" basis—seeking either individual or multi-issue agreements on Third World arms sales, conventional force reductions, cultural and scientific exchanges, human rights, emigration, communications, agricultural sales, energy, space, medicine, education, credits for Poland, environmental issues in the Pacific, the Bering Sea, the Arctic and the atmosphere; the potential list is staggering.

Sakharov has rightly noted that the prevention of war requires not only military but also "diplomatic, economic, ideological, political, cultural and social efforts." No one-party administration, fearful of being termed "soft on Russia" by the opposition, can give those other efforts a fraction of the time now devoted to the military aspect of this relationship. A Coalition Government, with bipartisan backing and no reelection concerns, could.

A new U.S.–U.S.S.R. agreement on trade and investment, replacing the 1973 treaty denounced by Moscow after the Jackson-Vanik amendments had con-

ditioned its implementation on Soviet emigration policies, could also be limited to the Coalition's four-year
term. No conditions on emigration or human rights
policies would then need to be formally attached to
this temporary pact; for no one could doubt that its
prospects for renewal in 1989 would depend upon
progress in those areas.

None of these potential agreements between the
superpowers will be easily reached or automatically
enforced. More than goodwill and earnest appeals,
more than high-level summits, more than formal or
highly publicized meetings, will be needed to move
the parties back from the brink of military confrontation. But four years of Coalition Government may offer
the best hope for giving Soviet-American relations, in
George Kennan's phrase, "a chance to breathe."

Genuine bipartisan backing for such an approach
will not be easily obtained. The polarization of American opinion on national security issues over the last
two decades has shattered the consensus within each
party as well as the nation. Combining the "doves" of
both parties on a single negotiating team will not be
enough. A superficially balanced approach that satis-
fies neither our legitimate security concerns nor the
need for meaningful arms control will not be enough.
The Coalition President, with the concurrence of the
Vice-President, must select for the most conspicuous
assignments men and women capable of gaining the
confidence of a broad spectrum of Congressional activ-
ists on both arms and arms control issues.

Distrust and discord, competition and conflicting
interests, will continue to be a part of the superpower

scene even when and if greater restraint and reciprocity have been achieved. Constructive coexistence between East and West will not ever be a simple or relaxed way of life. It is, in the words of Britain's Ambassador to Washington, Sir Oliver Wright, "merely better than any possible alternative—like war, cold war or capitulation."

# EPILOGUE

THE U.S.–Soviet relationship is not the only pressing international issue confronting the United States that should be removed from partisan politics. (The whole complex of issues affecting our relationship with Mexico has previously been cited as a prime example.) Nor are the Budget deficit, foreign competition, Third World debt and international trade barriers the only pressing economic issues that Coalition Government will need to address. No administration can limit its efforts to a preselected list of problems.

But these are the issues that must receive priority. These are the issues that justify now America's first experiment in Coalition Government, the issues that will otherwise continue to resist solution under present conditions of political gridlock and that can, unresolved, threaten our very way of life.

To be sure, we are not now actively engaged in fighting a civil war, as Lincoln was in 1864 when he chose Johnson, or suppressing domestic violence, as Colombia was in 1958 when it inaugurated the National Front Coalition. Nor are we actively engaged in

[ 131 ]

fighting an international war, as Franklin Roosevelt was in the early 1940s when he returned to bipartisanship in foreign policy, or as David Lloyd George was in 1916 when he led Britain's Coalition of National Unity. But we do face international and economic problems too ominous for us to risk recurring impotence in the Presidency, a growing lack of national confidence and consensus, and a continuing deadlock in relations between the two parties, between the two houses of Congress, and between the Executive and Legislative branches of our government. This nation has encountered such stalemates before. But our dangers now are too great to risk another Taylor-Fillmore-Pierce-Buchanan era or even another Hoover Administration.

Coalition Government is no panacea for the issues cited or any of the other ills that beset our nation. Like any new experiment, it may fail. It may worsen the political deadlock in Washington, producing a President and Vice-President who are not on speaking terms or a Cabinet and Administration paralyzed by divisiveness and plagued by unauthorized disclosures. Those who propose it may be ridiculed from the outset as impractical radicals or dreamers or denounced after it has been attempted for aggravating our problems. But I believe we should try.

If one or more Presidential candidates in either or both parties can adopt this basic course, if our political leadership can devote to bipartisan coalition and compromise the same effort and energy they have devoted to partisan confrontation and combat, if the American people can channel their disgust with present partisan excess and political deadlock into support for this unfamiliar but sensible approach, I believe it can work.

Nothing written or proposed in this book diminishes the importance of the individual elected to serve in the Oval Office. The wrong President will be unable to make Coalition or any other plan work effectively. The right President may be able to win enough confidence and build a sufficient consensus without some parts of this book's Coalition proposal. But a formal, full-scale plan has been presented here for any candidate in either party who may be interested in all or some of its parts.

The foregoing pages make clear that I am not seeking an end to political debate or party organization. I am not asking anyone to abandon his party or his principles. I am not expecting any Presidential candidate to embrace my every word. I am hoping that the necessary vision and courage and selflessness to consider and accept the fundamental thesis of this book will be demonstrated by at least one candidate and party and preferably by more than one. I am hoping that all those who read this book or hear its thesis will also consider what we all can do as private citizens to advance the cause of Coalition and the spirit of bipartisanship.

Political leaders will place the national good ahead of their individual and party ambitions, and endorse a temporary Coalition, only when a clear and vocal majority of voters recognizes those same priorities. Thus this message is addressed not only to politicians but to all concerned citizens. Its purpose is to stimulate thoughts about the unthinkable, to demonstrate the possibilities of the impossible, to suggest alternatives for which there are no precedents. It is written with the firm conviction that the American people will welcome an opportunity to break the present political deadlock and will respond favorably to a candidate who is willing to try.

For the American voter today does not place party ahead of basic principle. To paraphrase Jefferson: We are all democrats; we are all republicans.

*About the Author*

Since graduating from the University of Nebraska and its College of Law in 1951 in his home town of Lincoln, Nebraska, Ted Sorensen has divided his time between the worlds of government and law, frequently writing and lecturing about both.

After two early Washington assignments, he served for eleven years—eight years in the United States Senate and three years as Special Counsel to the President—as principal adviser on legislation and policy to John F. Kennedy. A member of the Executive Committee of the National Security Council, he was termed in the press Kennedy's "intellectual blood bank" and "alter ego."

Since 1966 Mr. Sorensen has been a senior partner in the New York law firm of Paul, Weiss, Rifkind, Wharton and Garrison. According to published reports about the firm, he specializes in international business and government transactions and in Washington regulatory matters, and has in that connection frequently been called upon to advise or represent the leaders of various foreign countries.

Mr. Sorensen and his wife and daughter live in New York City. Three grown sons live in the Midwest. He is reported to be an avid tennis player, moviegoer and opera fan. He is the author of five books and numerous articles, but the writing he claims to enjoy most is light verse that he composes for various family occasions.